The Quantity Theory of Money: A New Restatement

About IEA publications

The IEA publishes scores of books, papers, blogs and more – and much of this work is freely available from the IEA website: www.iea.org.uk

To access this vast resource, just scan the QR code below – it will take you directly to the IEA's Research home page.

THE QUANTITY THEORY OF MONEY: A NEW RESTATEMENT

TIM CONGDON

First published in Great Britain in 2024 by
The Institute of Economic Affairs
2 Lord North Street
Westminster
London SW1P 3LB
in association with London Publishing Partnership Ltd
www.londonpublishingpartnership.co.uk

The mission of the Institute of Economic Affairs is to improve understanding of the fundamental institutions of a free society by analysing and expounding the role of markets in solving economic and social problems.

Copyright © The Institute of Economic Affairs 2024

The moral rights of the authors have been asserted.

All rights reserved. Without limiting the rights under copyright reserved above, no part of this publication may be reproduced, stored or introduced into a retrieval system, or transmitted, in any form or by any means (electronic, mechanical, photocopying, recording or otherwise), without the prior written permission of both the copyright owner and the publisher of this book.

A CIP catalogue record for this book is available from the British Library.

ISBN 978-0-255-36842-1

Many IEA publications are translated into languages other than English or are reprinted. Permission to translate or to reprint should be sought from the Executive Director at the address above.

Typeset in Kepler by T&T Productions Ltd
www.tandtproductions.com

Printed and bound by Page Bros

CONTENTS

About the author	ix
Preface	x
Acknowledgements	xii
Summary	xiv
List of tables and figures	xvii

Introduction		1
	Focus on the transmission mechanism	4
	Different 'monetarisms'	10
	IS-LM – or IS vs. LM?	12
	Dangers of three-equation New Keynesianism	16
	Classroom gadgets vs. policy-relevant theory	19
1	**Setting the scene**	23
	The equation of exchange	23
	Need for a new restatement	26
2	**The Fisher equation: rights and wrongs**	28
	The case for broad money	28
	Transactions or national income?	31
3	**How is money created?**	35
	A fiat-money economy	35
	Two approaches	38
	Money-issuers vs. money-holders	40

4 The monetary theory of national income and wealth — 45

Money held in wealth portfolios — 47
The important notion of 'liquidity' — 49
The 'identification problem' — 50
Key statements: but is disequilibrium prevalent? — 51

5 The transmission mechanism: direct effects in 'the goods market' — 54

The black-box allegation — 55
Prices respond to change in money — 58
The proportionality postulate — 60
Inside money vs. outside money — 62
Is bank credit so special? — 68

6 The transmission mechanism: indirect effects via asset markets — 73

Variable-income assets vs. fixed-income assets — 74
Proportionality postulate applies to variable-income assets — 76
Textbooks' obsession with 'the rate of interest' — 79
Variable-income assets dominate bonds — 83
Lags between money and inflation — 87

7 Some evidence for the quantity theory of money — 90

US households in the long run — 91
A more international perspective — 92
The US over the medium term — 93
Summarising the evidence — 96

8	**Applying the theory to the US in the early 2020s**	**99**
	Covid shatters monetary equilibrium	100
	Money explosion	102
	Risks of double-digit inflation	106
	Fed chairman denies that 'money matters'	107
9	**Applying the theory to the UK in the early 2020s**	**109**
	The Great Stabilisation of the 2010s	109
	The Covid shock	111
	Official worries in early 2021 about *de*flation!	113
	Haldane's dissent	117
	Too much money chasing too few assets	118
	Too much money chasing too few goods	121
	The Great Destabilisation	124
	Who was to blame?	127
	Did the Bank have a theory of inflation?	129
10	**How this restatement differs from Friedman's**	**132**
	Unreliable base money multiplier	133
	Blatant assault on market economy	134
	Friedman's vacillations on money aggregate	136
11	**Conclusion: the quantity theory's continuing relevance and analytical power**	**140**
	A necessary and sufficient condition?	140
	Did Keynes end up 'hating' the quantity theory?	142

Appendix to Chapter 8 144

The contents of a special e-mail sent out on 30 March
2020 on 'Money trends in the US in 2020' 144

References 149

About the IEA 160

ABOUT THE AUTHOR

Tim Congdon is an economist and businessman. For almost 50 years, he has been a consistent advocate of free markets and sound money in the UK policy debate. One of his themes is that banking and money growth have powerful influences on macroeconomic outcomes. He is currently chair of the Institute of International Monetary Research, which he founded in 2014. The Institute is based at the University of Buckingham, where he is a professor of economics.

He was a member of the Treasury Panel of Independent Forecasters (the so-called 'wise persons') between 1992 and 1997, which advised the Chancellor of the Exchequer in a successful period for UK economic policy. He has been an advocate of money targeting to control inflation (and deflation) since his first job as an economic journalist on *The Times* between 1973 and 1976. He worked in the City of London from 1976 to 2005, where he explained the implications of macroeconomic trends for securities prices and asset allocation. He set up the influential consultancy, Lombard Street Research (now TS Lombard), in 1989.

PREFACE

This book began as the intended first chapter of another book – to be called *Money and Inflation at the Time of Covid* – which Edward Elgar Publishing plans to bring out in 2025. In the original version of about 23,000 words it was distributed in December 2023 as an attachment to the monthly e-mail I write for the Institute of International Monetary Research (mv-pt.org). Happily, Tom Clougherty, just appointed as Executive Director of the Institute of Economic Affairs, saw the e-mail and liked the attachment. He suggested that the chapter might become a short book in its own right, under IEA covers. I leapt at the idea. Within a few weeks, the 23,000 words had doubled and evolved into 11 chapters, and here is the result. I think it is coherent as a book, but readers can make up their own minds.

The IEA's intervention was appropriate for two reasons. First, in spring 2020 it had welcomed a contribution – entitled *Inflation: The Next Threat?* – on the then money explosion and the implied inflation risks from my colleague, Juan Castañeda, and me. Our worries in that publication have been amply vindicated in practice, and it is appropriate for the IEA to support a somewhat more analytical sequel. Second, in 2005 the IEA published my study of *Money and Asset Prices in Boom and Bust*, which reflected particularly my experiences – as a business economist and financial commentator – of the UK's two big boom–bust cycles in the 1970s and 1980s, and the calmer period which followed. The current work resumes the argument of *Money and Asset Prices in Boom and Bust*. Although I hark back to the beginnings of the quantity theory of money, this work is obviously a response to very recent events. The underlying theoretical framework is nevertheless the same in *The Quantity Theory of Money: A New Restatement* as in *Money and Asset Prices in Boom and Bust*. I hope it is organised and presented better.

ACKNOWLEDGEMENTS

I have several debts. First, the IEA has welcomed my research for many years, and – as I say in the introduction – I must express my gratitude to Tom Clougherty and Syed Kamall, who was the IEA's Editorial Director in 2020. Kristian Niemietz, now the IEA's Editorial Director and Head of Political Economy, has taken this publication forward and 'thank you'. Samuel Demeulemeester and John Greenwood read an early draft, and offered very helpful and detailed comments.

It will be clear from the book itself that I am no fan of most contemporary macroeconomists. All the same, the late Victoria Chick, Charles Goodhart and David Laidler have been on similar wavelengths to me throughout my career, even if not on exactly the same waveband. I have much valued their interest and support. Steve Hanke of Johns Hopkins University has become an outstanding proponent of broad-money monetarism, and I admire and thank him for battling with the reprobates who dominate the American profession.

Keynes's biographer, Lord Skidelsky, in his 2018 book *Government and Money* gave me the label and brand of 'Keynesian monetarist', which I like. I am indebted to him for that perhaps accidental exercise in promotion.

Finally, my colleagues at the Institute of International Monetary Research – especially Juan Castañeda and John Petley – have tolerated me in the last decade or so, and again 'thank you'. Fellow members of the IEA's Shadow Monetary Policy Committee have also been very easy-going and nice to me, even when I have been too much of a prima donna.

In preparing the book for publication, I am indebted to Jon Wainwright of T&T Productions for his help with reading and correcting an often awkward proof.

None of the above are responsible for the mistakes and infelicities which remain in *The Quantity Theory of Money: A New Restatement*. The restatement is in many ways a rather personal contribution, and I am very much to blame for its errors.

(I have a small style point. The first person is used in this preface and the introduction, but in the following chapters I refer to myself in the third person as 'the author'. The point may seem pedantic, but something has to be done for consistency.)

SUMMARY

- The overwhelming majority of economists were wrong in their forecasts about the consequences of the Covid-19 pandemic. They believed that it would result in years of falling inflation or even deflation. Instead, 2022 saw the highest inflation for 40 years in several leading economies.
- In early 2022, Professor Jason Furman, an influential American economist who advised President Obama, lamented the economics profession's 'dismal performance' and 'collective failure'.
- However, from an early stage those few economists who tracked a broadly defined measure of money – including the author of this book – correctly forecast the inflation flare-up. They noticed that in spring and summer a money supply explosion was under way in the US, the euro zone and the UK, and indeed in many other jurisdictions.
- This book argues that the high inflation numbers of 2022 and early 2023 were *caused* by excessive growth of the quantity of money. The Covid-related inflation episode was yet another illustration of Milton Friedman's adage that 'inflation is always and everywhere a monetary phenomenon'.

- Leading central banks – the Federal Reserve in the US, the European Central Bank in the euro zone, the Bank of England in the UK, and so on – organised the central bank asset purchases of long-dated securities from non-banks (or 'quantitative easing') which led to 2020's money explosion. They were therefore responsible for annual inflation peaking, after a fairly standard lag of about two years, at close to or above 10% in many countries.
- Different versions of the quantity theory of money – and of its modern incarnation as 'monetarism' – need to be distinguished. Meanwhile the equation of exchange ($MV = PT$) suffers from ambiguity and imprecision.
- This study emphasises the importance of a broadly defined money aggregate in the determination of nominal national income and wealth. It differs from Chicago School monetarism by denying that the monetary base and narrow money play a major causative role in a modern economy.
- The proportionality postulate – which nowadays is the claim of similar changes *in equilibrium* of broad money and nominal national income – is a reasonable approximation to the facts, although it needs to be qualified by 'financialisation'. This is the tendency for financial transactions (and hence the need for money) to grow faster than income as economies progress.
- In practice and for much of the time, most economies suffer from a degree of 'monetary disequilibrium'. (See chapters 4 and 5 for an explanation of this term.)

- Broad money may change substantially, and disruptively, in a particular period, shattering a previous monetary equilibrium. (The Covid-related events of 2020 were a good example.) If the quantity of money is then given for the next few periods, national income and wealth – along with the prices of goods and services, and of assets – have to change to restore equilibrium. Excess or deficient money *causes* these adjustments.
- The most important assets in the adjustment processes are corporate equity, housing and other forms of property, which have varying income over time. Bonds are relatively unimportant, even though they are the focus of discussion in macroeconomics textbooks.
- Indeed, many textbooks – notably the Samuelson textbook, which first appeared in 1948 with a condensation of Keynes's 1936 *General Theory* – adopt Keynes's liquidity preference theory of 'the rate of interest' (that is, a bond yield). They give this theory (and the associated 'IS function') an inappropriately large status in national income determination.
- In macroeconomic analysis the proportionality postulate can be assumed to apply to variable-income assets in equilibrium.
- Interest-rate-only macroeconomics – particularly as exemplified in the three-equation version of New Keynesianism – has ostracised money from central bank research in the twenty-first century. This kind of money-less macroeconomics is the key intellectual mistake behind the 'dismal performance' and 'collective failure' identified by Furman.

TABLES AND FIGURES

Table 1	Transactions through major US non-cash payments systems in 2021	31
Table 2	Value and composition of US household wealth at the end of 2021	48
Table 3	Money, income and the value of variable-income assets in the US, 1946–2021	77
Table 4	Capital gains and losses on variable-income assets in the US's Covid period	82
Table 5	Capital gains and losses on major asset classes in the US's Covid period	83
Table 6	Changes in US household sector balance sheet, 1946–2021	91
Table 7	Decadal growth rates of money and nominal GDP in the US from 1960	95
Table 8	The stability of the growth rates of money and nominal GDP in the US in the twentieth and twenty-first centuries	101
Table 9	The arithmetic of the US's 2020 money explosion	104

Figure 1	Corporate profits as a share of US GDP	76
Figure 2	Money growth and inflation in the G20, 1980–2022	94
Figure 3	Three-month annualised growth rate % of M3 broad money in the US, 2009 to mid 2020	106
Figure 4	Labour shortages, as seen by UK business, 1961–2022	123

INTRODUCTION

Economists in the mass – as a profession, no less – have not covered themselves in glory in the early 2020s. Like everyone, they were caught off guard by the Covid pandemic. But, unlike most people in other walks of life, they blundered in their reaction to it. An almost unanimous consensus was that Covid-19 would lead to years of disinflation and perhaps even of deflation. Instead, in 2022 inflation reached the highest levels for 40 years in the UK, as in other leading nations.

Economists in the US had a conspicuously bad record in their mis-forecasting of inflation. In January 2022, an influential figure in American policymaking, Professor Jason Furman of Harvard University, contributed a column to the Project Syndicate website, under the title, 'Why did almost nobody see inflation coming?' As he pointed out, in 2020 none of the Federal Open Market Committee's 18 members expected inflation above 2.5% in 2021. In fact, consumer prices rose by 7% in the year to December 2021. Furman lamented economists' 'dismal performance' and 'collective failure'.[1]

---

1   Few American economists are closer to economy policymaking than Furman, who was chairman of President Obama's Council of Economic Advisers from August 2013 to January 2017. At the time of writing (March 2024), he is the Aetna Professor of the Practice of Economic Policy jointly at Harvard Kennedy School and the Department of Economics at Harvard University.

But in the UK at least there were exceptions to Furman's 'collective failure'. I am pleased to say that they included me, the author of this short book.[2] Right from the start, in late March and April 2020, my assessment was that the astonishing money explosion then under way would have inflationary consequences. The first result would be too much money chasing too few assets, so that the prices of shares and houses would be buoyant in late 2020 and 2021; the second would be too much money chasing too few goods and services. Consumer inflation might reach double digits at an annual rate per cent in 2022 or 2023. I was particularly concerned about the inflation prospect in the US, although I did not neglect the UK and worried about the euro zone as well.[3] On 30 March 2020 I sent out a special e-mail to subscribers of the Institute of International Monetary Research monthly note. It ended with the sentence:

> Assuming that money growth does reach the 15 per cent to 20 per cent band [in the US] for a few months, the

---

[2] In the US the first notable economist to forecast more inflation was Steve Hanke at Johns Hopkins University. His close colleague, John Greenwood of International Monetary Monitor, contributed to a joint effort on this front. Greenwood and Hanke are kindred spirits, and we often work together, but their inflation warnings in this episode were a bit later than those from Castañeda and myself. Hanke's position in the debate was noticed by Jennifer Burns in her recent biography of Friedman (Burns 2023: 471).

[3] Congdon (2023a) covered the UK and included sections – written by me in April 2020 – warning about double-digit inflation. The euro zone is one of the six jurisdictions which have money trends monitored by the Institute of International Monetary Research in its regular monthly e-mails to subscribers.

message from history is that the annual increase in consumer prices will climb towards the 5 per cent – 10 per cent area and could go higher.

(The peak rate of annual money growth in fact came in June 2020, at over 25%. The full e-mail is reproduced in an appendix to chapter 8 below.) On 23 April 2020 the *Wall Street Journal* published an article by me with the headline warning 'Get ready for the return of inflation'. These two pieces were only a modest fraction of my output at the time (see, for example, Congdon 2020).

I collaborated closely with my colleague, Juan Castañeda, in the preparation of a pamphlet for the Institute of Economic Affairs called *Inflation: The Next Threat?* (Castañeda and Congdon 2020).[4] To quote from the synopsis:

> The extremely high growth rates of money [now being observed] will instigate an inflationary boom ... Central banks seem heedless of the inflation risks inherent in monetary financing of the growing government deficits.

The Institute of Economic Affairs is to be thanked for publishing our work very quickly, in June 2020. The then Editorial Director, Syed Kamall (now Lord Kamall), knew that we represented a minority view, but he backed us to

---

[4] I set up the Institute of International Monetary Research in 2014 and was its first Director. It is located at the University of Buckingham in England, where it helps in the post-graduate teaching of economics. Castañeda was appointed as the second Director in 2016, when I became the Institute's Chair.

the hilt. We are most grateful to him for his support. As noted in the acknowledgements, I must also thank most warmly Tom Clougherty, the IEA's current Director, for suggesting to me that this book – initially intended as the first chapter of a longer study on *Money and Inflation at the Time of Covid* – might make a worthwhile IEA publication.[5]

Focus on the transmission mechanism

The purpose of the current work is mostly to offer an analytical framework – a theory, if you wish – which explains why I was right in spring 2020 to predict a significant upturn in inflation. Another part of the agenda is to identify (what I regard as) a serious misperception in the majority thinking which led to economists' 'dismal performance'. My first step is to recall Milton Friedman's 1956 restatement of the quantity theory of money, as it is now almost seven decades later and another restatement is surely needed.

My focus is different from Friedman's. It is on the theory of the transmission mechanism from money to the economy, which in applied contexts usually means from changes in the rate of money growth to a range of macroeconomic outcomes. The outcomes include – crucially – the inflation rate. By contrast, in 1956 Friedman concentrated

---

5 This book is somewhat longer than the proposed first chapter of the book, *Money and Inflation at the Time of Covid*, but is much the same in content and argument. *Money and Inflation at the Time of Covid* is to be a collection of my writings in the early 2020s, which will be published by Edward Elgar Publishing in 2025.

on the properties of the money demand function. In explaining how money and the economy interact, I highlight the importance of an all-inclusive, broadly defined measure of money. Friedman would have sympathised with my approach, but he was never as fully committed to broad money as I am in this publication and have been throughout my career. Chapter 10 contains more detail on the differences between Friedman's position and the current restatement of the quantity theory.[6]

Chapters 5 and 6 are the vital ones in setting out the transmission mechanism; they should help in understanding how easy it was in spring 2020 to forecast the inflation flare-up which ensued over the next two to three years. My theoretical framework can be summarised in a box:

Main propositions of the restated quantity theory of money

1. Monetary equilibrium is established when non-bank private sector agents' demand to hold *all* money balances (i.e. broad money) is equal to the quantity of money created by the banking system and its customers.
2. When monetary equilibrium holds, the nominal levels of national income and wealth are at the levels desired by money-holding agents, and in that sense national income and wealth are determined.
3. Transactions are many times higher in value in a modern economy than national output. But – no matter how

---

[6] My position is also different from that of the Chicago School, of which Friedman was the most well-known member.

enormous their value – transactions between non-bank, money-holding agents cannot change an all-inclusive measure of the quantity of money. If monetary equilibrium does not hold and the quantity of money is given, national income and wealth must adjust to restore equilibrium.
4. Changes in the value of variable-income assets (equities, real estate) – often due to changes in the quantity of money – are a central feature of the transmission mechanism. The Keynesian claim that the transmission mechanism involves only changes in the value of bonds (i.e. in 'the rate of interest'), as in 'the IS function' of the textbooks, is a serious misunderstanding.
5. If certain assumptions are met, changes in the quantity of money and nominal national income are equi-proportionate in equilibrium ('the proportionality postulate'). In practice, the required assumptions are rarely met in full and 'monetary disequilibrium' often prevails. But enough stability is to be found in agents' money-holding behaviour, particularly in that of households, that changes in velocity (the inverse of the ratio of money to national income) are small over periods of several years. More exactly, they are small compared with changes in either broad money or national income.
6. In equilibrium, the proportionality postulate applies to variable-income assets, as well as to the goods and services which constitute national output.
7. The quantity of money is determined by the extension of credit to the state and the non-bank private sector by the banking system; it is not usefully interpreted as a

> simple multiple of cash issued by the central bank or of capital invested in banks. The banking system consists of both profit-motivated commercial banks and a central bank. The central bank has the unique prerogative of issuing legal-tender; its objectives are set out in legislation, which usually include the aim of price stability (or at any rate low inflation).

When shown this box, many economists may wonder what the fuss is all about. Don't the propositions amount to little more than organised common sense? Why has there been so much squabbling and rhetoric about these matters? Further, to the handful of economists who have bothered to read Keynes – as opposed to the hordes who call themselves 'Keynesians' – the contents of the box may be more than a little ironic. Monetarists and Keynesians are usually stereotyped as opposites or even antagonists. But the few authentic Keynesians, those who have read all his principal works and not just the *General Theory*, might contend that the box does no more than recall key themes in the 1930 *Treatise on Money*.

I would not resist this interpretation; Keynes – particularly the Keynes of the *Treatise*, and of the 1923 *Tract on Monetary Reform* and the vast body of still readable journalism – is one of my intellectual heroes. In his 2018 book on *Government and Money*, Keynes's biographer, Robert Skidelsky, labelled me a 'Keynesian monetarist' (Skidelsky 2018: 279–81). This may have bewildered people, as it seemed to be an oxymoron. I took it as a compliment. It does in fact locate me well in the much-disputed territories of macroeconomics and monetary theory. But I dislike intensely one salient theme in the *General Theory*, for reasons which will soon become apparent.

Skidelsky was kind enough to say in his book that my work was 'important', although he qualified this by describing me as 'lonely' and 'an outlier'. I regard my analytical framework as banal and straightforward, and do not believe it should be controversial. Nevertheless, the events of 2020 showed that Skidelsky was correct to suggest that I was an outlier. The framework implies – it very clearly and obviously implies – that a marked acceleration in the growth of broad money will result in a marked acceleration in inflation. But, to repeat, in spring 2020 – if close colleagues are excluded – I was almost in a minority of one in arguing that money growth in the teens or above per cent risked inflation in the teens per cent. Some attention was paid to my warnings, but not much.[7]

Frankly, the economics profession was hopeless in its initial assessment of the Covid-19 shock and the appropriate policy answers. The mistake was so bad that almost

---

[7] For example, Martin Wolf – in his *Financial Times* column on 20 May 2020 headed 'Why inflation might follow the pandemic' – referred to me, although keeping his distance. In his words:

> If one is a monetarist, like Tim Congdon, the combination of constrained output with rapid monetary growth forecasts a jump in inflation. But it is possible that the pandemic has lowered the velocity of circulation: people may hold this money, not spend it. But one cannot be certain. I will not forget the almost universally unexpected surge in inflation in the 1970s. This could happen again.

all economists were wrong about a major shift in the direction of change in the aggregate price level, less than 18 months before that shift occurred. In my view, the trouble stemmed, above all, from

- neglect of money growth trends in contemporary macroeconomic analysis, particularly in the supposed powerhouses of such analysis in the research departments of central banks, and
- imprecision, ambiguity and confusion in past statements of the quantity theory of money.

This book argues that the behaviour of money growth must be restored to a strategic position in policy-oriented macroeconomic analysis; it also tries to provide a statement of the quantity theory which is precise and rigorous, and therefore lends itself to successful forecasts of inflation.

When I use the phrase 'contemporary macroeconomic analysis', to which of its aspects am I most unsympathetic? This introduction may serve as an appetiser to the main course of the book's argument by emphasising two areas of particular disagreement and tension. One of these – which may come as a surprise – is with other economists who sometimes (or even always) say they are monetarists, adherents of the quantity theory or whatever; the other is with the pivotal position of the investment-saving (IS) function in textbook Keynesianism and a modish extension of textbook Keynesianism known as New Keynesianism.

Different 'monetarisms'

The main claims of this book rest on the ability of a broadly defined money aggregate to determine other macroeconomic variables. If this is monetarism, it is very much 'broad-money monetarism'. I am unenthusiastic about two alternative approaches, which might be called 'monetary-base monetarism' and 'narrow-money monetarism'. The subject is so large that concision risks misrepresentation, but space is limited, and I must be brief. The essence of these alternatives seems to me captured in the following descriptions:

> **Monetary-base monetarism.** This line of thought has two main versions. The first is that the monetary base *by itself* – without invoking any other money balances – is the key measure of money in the determination of national expenditure and income; the second is that the link between the monetary base and a deposit-dominated money aggregate is so mechanical and certain that their rates of change are similar (or even identical), and – via the influences of the base on the wider money aggregate and of the wider aggregate on the economy – the base is again the ultimate determinant of national expenditure and income.[8] (The monetary base is defined below in chapter 2; it consists of the monetary liabilities of the central bank.)
>
> **Narrow-money monetarism.** Here the idea is that a narrowly defined measure of money – again *by itself*

---

8   I have written a critique of the claim that the monetary base by itself determines spending and inflation (Congdon 2023b).

– determines national expenditure and income. By implication, the tracking of a narrow aggregate such as M1 is sufficient for the analyst to forecast inflation. Further, if exponents of the quantity theory are asked for evidence of stable money-holding preferences, they think M1 is the appropriate aggregate in econometric investigation. (Narrow money is also defined in chapter 2.)

I am antipathetic to much of what these two kinds of monetarism have to say. They have done a lot of damage. When adopted by distinguished and influential economists, they have often led to forecasting mistakes and embarrassment.

When Friedman made his 'blooper' on inflation in the 1980s, by forecasting a significant rise which did not occur, the blooper arose from his selection of M1 as the most important aggregate in assessing inflation trends[9]; when Patrick Minford in the late 1980s wrongly quarrelled with me about whether the UK's Lawson boom would prove inflationary, it was his attachment to the M0 notion of the monetary base which was responsible[10]; when four fellows

---

9   For Friedman's mistake on inflation, see Barnett (2012: 107–11). 'Blooper' is Friedman's own word. According to Jennifer Burns (2023: 441) in her Friedman biography, Friedman said to a journalist about his mistake, 'I was wrong, absolutely wrong. And I have no good explanation as to why I was wrong.' If he did say this, it was disturbing, to say the least. See the discussion in chapter 10.

10 The disagreement between Minford and myself was discussed in Congdon (1992: 126–28, 226–27). Minford had been influenced by Eugene Fama, a Nobel laureate who has taught at the University of Chicago for virtually all of his academic career. My views on Fama's monetary economics are given in chapter 5.

of the Hoover Institution signed an Open Letter to Ben Bernanke in 2010, with its misjudged warning that the Fed's asset purchases would cause 'currency debasement', they were anxious about the very rapid growth of the monetary base consequent on those asset purchases.[11] To reiterate, I do not care for either monetary-base monetarism or narrow-money monetarism. Moreover, I have no truck with appeals to 'the aggregates' in the plural, since these in my view are confessions of muddle or even ignorance. Analysis in this area of economics should relate to a broadly defined measure of money, full stop. Admittedly, there is a so-called 'boundary problem' in defining it.[12]

IS-LM – or IS vs. LM?

What is my objection to the IS function? Non-economist readers may be puzzled by the phrase. The IS function originated in a 1937 review article of Keynes's *General Theory*. It was written by Sir John Hicks, later awarded the Nobel Prize and undoubtedly one of Britain's greatest economists. (He is given a starring role in chapter 5 below.) The *General Theory* may have been a revolutionary work, but perhaps for this very reason it was difficult to

---

[11] For the Open Letter to Ben Bernanke, see https://www.hoover.org/research/open-letter-ben-bernanke. The forecast of rising inflation was completely wrong. In a 2014 column in the *New York Times*, Paul Krugman called the Open Letter 'infamous'. See 'Knaves, fools and Quantitative Easing', *New York Times*, 2 October 2014.

[12] Should broad money include only bank liabilities or liquid assets issued by non-banks? What about foreign currency deposits? For these issues in monetary economics, see Goodhart (2008).

follow and understand. Not the least of its perplexities was that 'the rate of interest' (meaning a bond yield) was active in two ostensibly separate processes of national income determination. The rate of interest *both* equilibrated the demand to hold money with the supply, where the demand to hold money was related to national income, *and* it determined investment, where national income was a multiple of investment.

Were there two distinct theories of national income determination in the one purported master work? Hicks's trick was to propose one function (which became 'the LM [liquidity preference–money supply] function') for the monetary component of Keynes's magnum opus, and another function ('the IS function') to represent the multiplier story. The two functions could be translated into equations, thereby becoming a simple simultaneous-equations model of the economy; they could also be assembled in an IS/LM diagram with two neatly intersecting curves. Keynes sent Hicks a postcard blessing the IS/LM construction. It has subsequently adorned over three generations of macroeconomics textbooks, with one of its attractions being that it is easy to mark in examinations.

But the IS/LM 'thing' (Hicks's later characterisation) depended on the structure of Keynes's argument in the *General Theory*, and in one important respect that structure was unrealistic to the point of crankiness.[13] In much of the *General Theory* Keynes restricted the choice between money

---

13 Hicks used the word 'thing' in the first sentence of a 1980 paper on 'IS-LM: an explanation'. The paper was reprinted as chapter 23 of Hicks (1982).

and assets to a choice between money and bonds.[14] Hence an increase in the quantity of money raised the price of bonds, which lowered bond yields and his 'rate of interest', which stimulated investment, which further spurred a gain in national expenditure and income that was a multiple of the extra investment. Here was the IS function at work.[15]

The last paragraph summarises a key strand in the *General Theory*; its sentences also respect syntax and the recognised meaning of words. However, in my view it is fantastic that this part of the *General Theory* has been

---

14 In fact, Keynes did not refer in the *General Theory* to the so-called direct effects of a change in the quantity of money on the economy. See footnote 1 to chapter 5 for the distinction between direct and indirect effects of changes in the quantity of money, as developed in Blaug (1985). A better sentence than the one in the text might be, 'In influential chapters of *The General Theory* Keynes implied that the only category in the economy with an important reaction to a change in the quantity of money was the value of a bond.' Rather obviously, that was not – and is not – right.

15 Unhappily, according to Keynes, circumstances could be imagined (of 'virtually absolute liquidity preference', in his words) where bond prices were already so high that investors had to expect the next major move in prices would be downwards (see Keynes 1973: 207). An increase in the quantity of money could therefore not raise bond prices, lower the rate of interest and stimulate the economy. Monetary policy could be condemned to ineffectiveness, justifying Keynes's advocacy of public works as a valid means of combating depression. It was this claim of monetary policy ineffectiveness which appealed to many left-leaning economists in the 1940s, 50s and 60s (when Soviet communism seemed to offer an alternative to market capitalism), and curiously still does so today (even though Soviet communism has been thoroughly discredited). They wanted monetary policy sidelined, so that economic policy could become dominated by fiscal policy (and higher government spending) and planning (with consequence intervention in private-sector business and finance). For these wider ramifications of Keynes's musings on 'absolute liquidity preference' (and the related 'liquidity trap' idea found in Keynesian textbooks), see, for example, Skousen (1992: 9–34).

accorded so much attention by three generations of economists. Is this the right way to organise the interpretation of business and financial reality? In the hypothetical world of the *General Theory* only two assets figure in the analysis, that is, money and bonds; in the real world, agents are balancing money both against goods and services, and an assortment of assets of which equities and real estate are far more important than bonds. As I discuss in chapters 2 to 6 in this book, and particularly in chapters 5 and 6, bonds are a relatively unimportant asset class in a modern economy. Fluctuations in the value of equities and real estate (which I call 'variable-income assets') have far greater effects on changes in aggregate demand than fluctuations in the value of bonds (fixed-income assets).

The IS function may have helped Hicks to summarise the complex argument of the *General Theory* for the purposes of university instruction. But this part of Keynes's larger thesis was – and remains – about a minor feature of the economy and has little traction in understanding modern business life. Given the trivial position of bonds in the household sector balance sheet (as shown in chapters 4 and 6), the IS function misses at least 90% of the interaction between money and the economy. Indeed, in the extreme conditions of late 2020 and early 2021, when excess money drove large gains in the stock market and house prices, it was probably picking up less than 2% of that interaction. (See pp. 82–87 in chapter 6 for more justification of this statement.)

The analytical logic behind the LM curve may be more elusive than that behind the IS curve, as it involves reasoning in sometimes abstruse areas of monetary economics. Further, if money has to be retained in macroeconomics, that means banks have to be brought into the analysis as well.[16] Banks have balance sheets, while some Keynesian economists seem to find balance sheets difficult to read and understand.[17] Over time the IS/LM approach has therefore been truncated and simplified into an approach with the IS function only.[18] A high proportion of today's macroeconomists have come to think in terms of an IS function – *and only an IS function* – when they want to determine aggregate demand and national income. They forget about money, in the sense of 'the quantity of money', altogether. In 2020, the year which in the US saw the fastest growth of broadly defined M3 money since World War II, the minutes of the Federal Open Market Committee contained not one reference to any money aggregate.[19]

Dangers of three-equation New Keynesianism

The airbrushing of money from economic analysis is most evident in the three-equation distillation of New

---

16 Bank deposits are the dominant kind of money nowadays.

17 Romer (2000: 162) complained about 'the confusing and painful analysis of how the banking system "creates" money.'

18 Romer (2000) illustrates the point.

19 In the US the Federal Reserve stopped publishing an M3 series in 2006. However, an independent consultancy, Shadow Government Statistics, continues to estimate M3 numbers from publicly available information, much of it from the Fed. I am grateful to Shadow Government Statistics for the data.

Keynesianism, a body of thought often deemed to be the workhorse of today's central bank research.[20] In this body of thought only one equation determines national expenditure and income, and it is indeed an IS function.[21] In qualification, the rate of interest in the three-equation model is not Keynes's bond yield, but the central bank rate.[22] The substitution is intended to enable the three-equation approach to inform real-world decision-taking by central banks, since it is widely agreed that the rate of interest – not the quantity of money – is their main policy instrument. (The monetarists have advocated following the quantity of money as an intermediate target; they have not said that the quantity of money is a policy instrument. However, operations such as asset purchases from or sales to *non-banks* have a fairly direct, measurable impact on the quantity of money.[23])

Despite the exclusion of money and banking from the three-equation framework, Huw Pill, the current chief

---

20 The word 'workhorse' – to describe the position of three-equation New Keynesianism in central bank research – is used on the cover of Galí (2008).

21 The ostracising of money – in the sense of the quantity of money – from macroeconomics has occurred particularly in the twenty-first century, with a key influence being the version of the three-equation New Keynesian model set out in the much-cited article, Clarida et al. (1999).

22 The use of the central bank rate in the IS function raises many questions. In my view the central bank rate equilibrates the demand for central bank credit with its supply, and it is set by transactions between the central bank and commercial banks. This is very different from the bond yield in Keynes's liquidity preference theory, which is set mostly by non-bank investors in the bond market, and brings together their demand to hold money with the quantity of money in existence (Congdon 2018).

23 The topic is covered in essay 4 in Congdon (2011). See, particularly, pp. 80–81 on different types of open market operation.

economist at the Bank of England, has said that this kind of New Keynesianism is 'canonical'.[24] One premise of chapters 5 and 6 of this book is, on the contrary, that three-equation New Keynesianism is worthless if it is intended to throw light on reality. In particular, the omission of money makes it difficult for central banks to calibrate the size of purchases or sales of long-dated assets (that is, 'quantitative easing' or 'quantitative tightening') when they want to influence the economy by this method. The asset purchases conducted in 2020 and 2021 were much too large in most of the world's leading economies. But as central banks did not think about the numerical consequences of their asset purchases for the quantity of money, and as they anyhow dismissed the macroeconomic significance of that quantity, they did not appreciate that a major rise in inflation became inevitable because of their actions.

Pill's apparent canonisation of the three-equation model is picked up and criticised in chapters 6 and 9. As it happens, the evidential basis for the IS function is underwhelming. Early in the twenty-first century Edward Nelson, one of the Federal Reserve's top economists and an assiduous reader of the academic journals, was well aware of the rise of three-equation New Keynesianism. But he had had a few brushes with the data and proposed that there was an 'IS puzzle'. New Keynesians might say an IS function was one of their crucial three equations, but in the real world the IS function was a bit of a sphinx; it did

---

24 Pill (2022a) used the word 'canonical' more than once in his approval of three-equation New Keynesianism.

not have the form or the properties it was supposed to have. A notable contribution was made by Charles Goodhart and Boris Hofmann in a February 2005 article, on 'The IS curve and the transmission of monetary policy: is there a puzzle?', in the *Applied Economics* journal (Goodhart and Hofmann 2005). Like so many others, they found that work on reduced-form IS functions was unrewarding. Their best-fitting relationships usually had no explanatory power, but – when they did – all too often the coefficients on the interest rate term were wrongly signed or insignificant. To find better relationships, they added explanatory variables such as property prices and – intriguingly – a monetary aggregate.

Classroom gadgets vs. policy-relevant theory

One of the most active researchers on the IS function was Livio Stracca, an economist at the European Central Bank. In Stracca (2010), he wondered whether the travails of the IS function arose because too much attention had been paid to possibly perverse and misleading results for a limited number of countries. (He may have been thinking of the US and the UK in particular, as these tend to attract most attention from English-speaking economists, for obvious reasons.) He therefore assessed 'data from 22 OECD countries over 40 years'. His verdict was damning (Stracca 2010):

> I find little evidence in favour of the traditional specification [of the IS curve] where the real interest rate enters with a negative sign due to intertemporal substitution:

on the contrary, it is typically either insignificant or wrongly signed. Overall, I conclude that the New Keynesian IS curve, at least in its most common formulations, is not structural and is overwhelmingly rejected by the data.

The literature on the IS function is small, but enough work has been done to establish a definite conclusion: convincing relationships between the levels of interest rates and nominal GDP are hard to find, while those between changes in the two variables are yet more elusive. If the IS function is a vital element in a model viewed as fundamental, even canonical, in central bank research, something has gone badly wrong.

Moreover, the elusiveness of the relationship between interest rates and aggregate demand is hardly new. Friedman's long-time collaborator, Anna Schwartz (1987: 175), once offered a generalisation from her many years of research. Speaking at an academic conference in the UK in 1969, she said,

> The correlations between the level or rates of change in interest rates, on the one hand, and rates of change in nominal income, prices and output, on the other, are considerably worse than those between rates of change in the quantity of money and these magnitudes.

Of course, the structure of economies does change over the decades, but – when I tried to disprove Schwartz's generalisation by looking at the US data about 50 years later

– the data refused to comply. The Schwartz generalisation remains valid (Congdon 2021a).

This is not to dispute the potential value of the three-equation approach – like IS/LM – as a classroom gadget.[25] But, when economists leave the classroom and assume positions of significant policymaking power, such gadgets may not be much help. If non-economists want to understand why the economics profession has made a hash of the early 2020s, it is – in my view – the veneration of the IS function and the canonisation of three-equation New Keynesianism which deserve much of the blame. Interest-rate-only macroeconomics has become dominant in central bank practice, and expelled the quantity of money from research and analysis. Here is the main source of the intellectual failure behind, in Furman's words, the 'dismal performance' of economists in the early 2020s.

I admire the bulk of Keynes's contribution to macroeconomic theory, but in my view, he used several chapters of the *General Theory* – specifically, chapters 13–18 – to launch a misguided marketing exercise for the liquidity preference theory of the rate of interest. The IS curve, a by-product of that theory, was later given more prominence in Keynesian textbooks than it merited. This was a wrong turning. One ambition of the *Treatise on Money* was to develop a theory of the determination of the value of *all* non-liquid

---

25 The phrase 'classroom gadget' to describe the IS/LM 'thing' appears in the concluding section of Hicks's 1980 paper 'IS-LM: an explanation' (Hicks 1982).

assets, including securities other than bonds.[26] By contrast, a big chunk of the *General Theory* was preoccupied with an unimportant issue, the balance in portfolios between money and bonds. Curiously, and paradoxically, the *Treatise* in this respect – as in others – had greater generality than the more famous *General Theory*.[27]

---

26 The prefaces to the foreign editions of Keynes's *Treatise* contained the following statement (Keynes 1971: xxvii):

> My central thesis regarding the determination of the price of non-liquid assets is that, given a) the quantity of inactive deposits offered by the banking system, and b) the degree of the propensity to hoard or state of bearishness, then the price level of non-liquid assets must be fixed at whatever figure is required to equate the quantity of hoards which the public will desire to hold at that price level with the quantity of hoards which the banking system is creating.

More succinctly, the price level of non-money assets depends on the quantity of money and wealth-holders' money-holding preferences. Keynes even ventured a remark on house prices. To quote (p. xxvi):

> When a man in a given state of mind is deciding whether to hold bank deposits or house property, his decision depends not only on the degree of his propensity to hoard, but also on the price of house property.

27 Another illustration is that the *Treatise* has both a central bank and a commercial banking system, with the central bank issuing base money and the commercial banks bank deposits. By contrast, the *General Theory* has a consolidated banking system which issues money. One result of the simplification is that the *General Theory* has no well-developed account of the determination of the quantity of money.

1   SETTING THE SCENE

Views on an economy's future – on the outlook for growth, employment and inflation – depend on the theory of national income held by the people who propose them, as well as the facts of the conjunctural situation. This book appeals to and develops a traditional approach to the subject which comes under the label 'the quantity theory of money'.[1] An argument is put forward that the quantity theory – or at any rate a version of it – is basic to understanding the inflation flare-up of the 2020s.

The equation of exchange

The main features of the theory are so well-established that they received quite detailed treatment in a

---

1   At one time the quantity theory of the value of money was contrasted with the cost-of-production theory of the value of money, which was related to the labour theory of value. This contrasting made sense when money took mostly metallic form, but is obviously anachronistic in a fiat-money economy. See part 4, 'The exchange value of money', in Wicksell (1935), translated from Swedish by E. Classen. (The *Lectures* had originally been published in Swedish in two volumes in 1903 and 1906.) Wicksell judged that the quantity theory was 'the only one which can make any claim to real scientific importance' (p. 141). Notice that Wicksell's discussion preceded Irving Fisher's 1911 *The Purchasing Power of Money*.

sixteenth-century work by the French philosopher, Jean Bodin (1530–96).[2] Its central proposition is the so-called 'equation of exchange', a standard item in hundreds of textbooks. The most familiar form of the equation runs as follows:

$MV = PT,$

where M is the quantity of money, V the velocity of circulation, P the price level and T the volume of transactions. The equation of exchange is sometimes described as a truism or even as an identity, where the two sides of the equation are the same because of how its terms are defined. Milton Friedman (1912–2006) became famous in the late twentieth century for advancing a related set of policy recommendations carrying the label of 'monetarism'.[3] He is often considered the foremost modern exponent of the quantity theory of money. At one point he even compared the role of the equation of exchange in economics to that of the Einstein formula for mass–energy equivalence ($E = mc2$) in physics (Friedman 1992: 39).[4]

---

[2] Jean Bodin's *La réponse aux paradoxes de Malestroit* (1568) is covered in many histories of economic thought. An English translation was published in Bodin (1997).

[3] Arguably, monetarism comes in different shapes and sizes, and several versions can be differentiated. In a 1987 paper, the author suggested that the 'American monetarism' of, in particular, the Chicago School was different from 'British monetarism', the brand of monetarism which was important in inflation control in Britain in the late 1970s and early 1980s. See essay 13 in Congdon (2011).

[4] Samuel Demeulemeester has pointed out to the author that – in *The Purchasing Power of Money* – Fisher likened the equation of exchange to Boyle's law of gases, that is, the pressure of a given quantity of gas varies with its

Friedman acknowledged his intellectual debt to Irving Fisher, a professor at Yale University from 1898 to 1935, and an influential figure until his death in 1947. It was Fisher's 1911 book on *The Purchasing Power of Money* which proselytised the $MV = PT$ formula in the then quite new academic discipline of economics, and $MV = PT$ is often known as 'the Fisher equation'.[5] The young John Maynard Keynes, who had only recently been appointed to a lectureship in economics at Cambridge University, reviewed Fisher's book for the *Economic Journal*. (The *Economic Journal* is the flagship publication of the Royal Economic Society, and it was then – and still is today – the leading economics publication in the UK for university teachers.) Keynes's review was mostly friendly, and the book undoubtedly made a deep impression on him. Nevertheless, Keynes later said that much of his intellectual evolution was 'a long struggle to escape' from the incumbent doctrines of his early adulthood, which included the quantity theory. Towards the end of the twentieth century, Mark Blaug, an historian of economic thought, put it more sharply. In his words, 'Keynes began by loving [the quantity theory of money], but ended by hating it' (Blaug et al. 1995: 1). (An assessment of the matter by Keynes's biographer, Robert Skidelsky, was more restrained.)[6] The three names

---

volume at a constant temperature. Boyle's law was given mathematical expression as early as the late seventeenth century. Is it unfair to suggest that economists suffer from physics envy?

5   Fisher did not originate the equation which carries his name. Credit for that is usually given to Simon Newcomb (1836–1909), a remarkable American polymath whose main interest was in astronomy.

6   See Robert Skidelsky's 'J. M. Keynes and the quantity theory of money' in Blaug et al. (1995: 80–95), particularly the section at the top of p. 83.

– Fisher, Keynes and Friedman – recur on many occasions in the following pages.

Need for a new restatement

Despite its distinguished pedigree, the equation of exchange is beset by ambiguity and imprecision, and in its familiar unadorned version has to be rejected as unsatisfactory. The quantity theory of money demands a clearer and more robust restatement. Friedman made an attempt to provide such a restatement in the opening chapter to *Studies in the Quantity Theory of Money*, published by the University of Chicago Press (Friedman 1956: 3–21). The 1956 book is sometimes seen as an example of the sort of work at which the so-called Chicago School excelled in its heyday. As is celebrated or deplored (depending on one's point of view), the hallmarks of Chicago School thinking were support for free-market capitalism and advocacy of monetary stability to help capitalism work better (see Emmett 2010).[7]

The current book can be seen partly as a response to the many challenges faced by the quantity theory, and indeed by 'monetarism', in the seven decades since Friedman's restatement. Its content and theses differ from Friedman's in fundamental respects. The challenges to the quantity theory have been miscellaneous, over a wide front and large

---

7 In 1977 Friedman retired from the University of Chicago, after teaching there for 30 years, and moved to San Francisco. The distinctive Chicago tradition of monetary economics now lies in the past and is only a matter of historical record.

in number. An attempt to reply to them risks being untidy and repetitive. To maintain a consecutive argument, much of the action is relegated to and takes place in the book's footnotes. This is not ideal, but our key aim – to throw light on the recent Covid-related business cycle, and the impact of money growth on the high inflation of 2022 and 2023 – must be remembered.

Back in 1956 Friedman was particularly concerned with the properties of agents' demand to hold money (or the so-called 'demand for money function'). The emphasis here is rather on the characteristics and attainment of 'monetary equilibrium', a condition in which the demand to hold money is equal to the quantity of money in being. Discussion of monetary equilibrium, and the transmission mechanism from changes in the quantity of money to macroeconomic outcomes, takes up five crucial chapters, from chapters 2 to 6. Chapter 7 provides evidence for the quantity theory. Chapter 8 applies the theory to the circumstances of the American economy in the early 2020s, and explains how the quantity theory scored a major success by forecasting – several quarters in advance – the inflation upturn of late 2021 and 2022. Chapter 9 carries out much the same exercise, but relates to the UK economy. The differences between Milton Friedman's monetary economics and the broad-money monetarism in the current work are covered in chapter 10. The final chapter insists on the continuing analytical power and policy relevance of quantity-theory thinking.

2 THE FISHER EQUATION: RIGHTS AND WRONGS

The equation of exchange may be in the shop window of the quantity theory, as it is usually presented. But it is loosely formulated, and has been widely criticised as ambiguous and unsatisfactory. Its first ambiguity arises because money can be defined in more than one way. Thus, 'the quantity of money' is occasionally said to consist only of liabilities of the central bank – that is, the note issue and banks' cash reserves – and is thereby equated with 'the monetary base' (for an example, see Sumner 2021: 45). The practice even extends to top central bankers when they equate monetary policy exclusively with actions affecting the size of the central bank balance sheet. But a focus on the central bank balance sheet cannot be the whole story, because only a miniscule proportion of transactions is completed with notes, and banks' own expenditure is a small part of aggregate demand. (The author emphasised the point in Congdon (2023b), particularly section 3, pp. 189–91.)

The case for broad money

More plausible definitions include bank deposits, since the overwhelming majority of payments in today's world use deposits. Two types of definition then come into contention: those that include only deposits (sight deposits in the US, current accounts in the UK) which can be used without giving any notice, and those that include all, or virtually all, deposits (time deposits in the US, deposit accounts in the UK).[1] Definitions including only immediately accessible deposits are said to refer to 'narrow money', whereas those that include all, or virtually all, deposits are 'broad money'.

In the rest of this book the phrase 'the quantity of money' should always be understood to mean 'broad money'. The rationale for downplaying the monetary base and narrow money will become easier to understand as the book's contents are presented. However, the essence of the matter is straightforward. Basic to the book's analytical framework is that – if money is out of kilter with agents' expenditure decisions and asset portfolios – it is the expenditure decisions and asset portfolios that adjust, not the other way round.

But this is not true with narrow money. If my sight deposit is too large relative to my expenditure and assets, I can change it by transferring the excess to another type of deposit, probably one that pays interest and can be withdrawn only after giving notice. (In a phrase to be recalled

---

[1] Drawing the boundary between bank deposits definitely inside an all-inclusive money measure and just outside is often difficult. Should foreign currency deposits be included? What about deposits with a long term to maturity? Are balances to be included if they are liabilities of a banking-type institution which does not belong to a settlement system? Monetary economics is not an easy subject.

near the book's end, I can change it by a 'money transfer'.) Both my own sight deposits, and the aggregate level of narrow money in the economy, can therefore alter in response to the relative attractiveness of different kinds of deposit within the broad money total, as well as the wider economic background. When narrow money does alter in this way, it does not reflect or affect money-holders' decisions on expenditure and portfolios, and it is such decisions that impact on the economy as a whole and matter in macroeconomic analysis.

By contrast, if all my bank deposits are too large relative to my expenditure and assets, I have to spend more on goods and services, or acquire more assets, to eliminate the excess. An all-inclusive measure of money is not changed by shifts in the relative size of its components. Indeed, as a matter of logic, it cannot be changed by such compositional shifts. Broad money – not the monetary base or narrow money – must be the aggregate which figures in a convincing monetary theory of national income.[2] To summarise, the quantity of money can be regarded for most purposes – and certainly for the purposes of the present study – as consisting of notes and coin held by the public and practically *all* the deposit liabilities of the banking system. Further, this book could be understood as exercises in – or even as a manifesto for – broad-money monetarism.

---

[2] The argument in the last few paragraphs was also made by the author in a 1990 paper reprinted in part 8 of Congdon (1992). See, in particular, pp. 179–83.

Table 1 Transactions through major US non-cash payments systems in 2021

Name of system	Description	Volume of transactions, in millions	Value of transactions, in $ trillions ('000s of billlions)	Average transaction size, $
Fedwire	Large-value, real time	204.5	991.8	4,849,878
CHIPS	Interbank settlement	127,900	448.7	3,508
FedACH	Includes direct debits	17,900	37.0	2,067
Electronic Payments Network ACH	Includes direct debits	29,100	72.6	2,495
Total value of all transactions through non-cash systems			1,550.1	

Source: US Department of the Treasury (2022: 9).

Transactions or national income?

The second ambiguity in the equation of exchange stems from the elusiveness of the notion of 'transactions' in the uncluttered $MV = PT$ version of the equation of exchange. Economists, and non-economists seeking advice from economists, are usually interested in national income and output, and the price level of output, and hence in their determinants. But the level of transactions in any economy is not at all the same thing as the level of national income and output. As Table 1 shows, transactions through settlement systems in the American economy had in 2021 a value of just above $1,550 trillion or more than 65 times nominal gross domestic product, which was $23.3 trillion in the year. Crucially, transactions are carried out in assets, while purchases and sales of *existing* assets are not part of the transactions in the so-called 'income–expenditure–output circular flow' which fix national income, expenditure and output in a direct and definitional sense. In his 1930 classic *Treatise on Money* Keynes said that transactions in assets took place in 'the financial circulation', while transactions in goods and services, plus such payments as those for factor services, belonged to 'the industrial circulation' (Keynes 1971: 48).

By implication, a distinction might be drawn between two formulations of the equation of exchange, one in terms of transactions, and the other in terms of national income. The transactions version can be presented as before, but with the subscript 't' added to both the velocity and price level terms:

$$MV_t = P_t T,$$

where V_t is called the 'transactions velocity of money' and P_t is a 'price level' which must contain the prices both of assets transacted in the financial circulation, and of goods and services transacted in the industrial circulation. But a price level which muddles up the prices of assets with the prices of goods and services would have little use. In his *Treatise*, Keynes derided it as 'a hotch-potch standard' which would prove 'unreliable as a guide to the Purchasing Power of Money' (Keynes 1971: 236). This was a jibe – a sharp and telling jibe – against Irving Fisher's 1911 book on the topic.

What about the formulation in terms of national income? Can that rescue the key ideas in the discussion? The same step is carried out as in the last paragraph, with the subscript 'y' added again to the velocity and price level terms, to give

$$MV_y = P_y Y,$$

where M continues to signify the quantity of money, V_y is known as 'the income velocity of circulation', P_y is the price level of the goods and services that enter national income/output, and Y is national income/output.

The phrase 'the income velocity of money' appears many times in Keynes's celebrated *The General Theory of Employment, Interest and Money*, whereas 'the transactions velocity of money' does not appear at all. Perhaps Keynes believed the P_y term to correspond to an analytically useful price level and, hence, that the income version of the equation of exchange was more useful than the transactions version. But arguably this gain has come at the cost of loosening the notion of 'velocity' from business reality. Few people would say that the purchase of a second- or third-hand car is intrinsically much different from that of a new car. However, only the value added in a new car is part of national output, because second- and third-hand cars were usually manufactured a few years ago. So the velocity of money deployed in used-car transactions does not affect 'the income velocity of money', whereas the velocity of money in new-car transactions does affect it. At one point in the *General Theory* Keynes protested against the income velocity notion. It was, he remarked, 'merely a name which explains nothing ... The use of [the] term obscures ... the real character of the causation, and has led to nothing but confusion' (Keynes 1973: 299).

This may have been going too far, but it warns against a mechanical application of the terms in the equation of exchange to real-world categories and issues. Chapter 4 develops a different approach to the quantity theory of money which largely reflects the objections of Keynes and his Cambridge colleagues to equation-of-exchange thinking. Before moving on, it has to be said that the terms in the equation of exchange cannot be entirely avoided. Velocity is an item of economists' mental furniture and occasionally they have to sit on it, even if it makes them uncomfortable.

3 HOW IS MONEY CREATED?

Friedman's 1956 restatement of the quantity theory asserted that it was 'in the first instance a theory of the demand for money. It is not a theory of output, or of nominal income or of the price level' (Friedman 1956: 4). This was a new and idiosyncratic departure, since many previous authorities had made confident assertions that the quantity theory was indeed about the relationship between money on the one hand, and nominal incomes and prices on the other (Blaug 1985: 690). A central purpose of the current restatement is to throw light on the monetary transmission mechanism, whereby *the demand to hold money* is matched up with the quantity of money (or *'the money supply'*). This chapter is concerned with the determination of the quantity of money in modern conditions, while the following three chapters are about the definition of monetary equilibrium and the monetary transmission mechanism as such.

A fiat-money economy

Since most of broad money consists of bank deposits, their creation must in some sense be the work of the banking system. But how exactly does money come into being? By what process or processes do banks introduce new money into the economy? In one of his theoretical papers Friedman ducked the issue by appealing to 'helicopter money', conjuring up a vision of bank notes falling from the sky (Friedman 1969: 4–5; 1992: 29–37). He may have wanted to recall the era when gold or silver were the principal monetary assets, and the quantity of money increased adventitiously – as if out of the sky – when new mines were discovered.

Nowadays money has ceased to be a commodity like a precious metal. Instead, virtually all money is a liability of banks, whether it takes the form of legal-tender notes issued by the central bank or of deposits issued by commercial banks.[1] In one sense the creation of new money in this sort of world, the world of so-called fiat money, is straightforward. Because the central bank's notes are legal tender and must be taken in payment, they can be increased by the simultaneous addition of identical sums to both sides of its balance sheet. Shockingly (or so it seems), new money comes out of 'thin air'. As Galbraith (1975: 29) remarked in *Money: Whence It Came, Where It Went*, 'The process by which money is created is so simple that the mind is repelled.'

At first glance commercial banks are in a similar position. People believe that payments can be made from bank deposits, as long experience has established that this is

---

[1] A trivial exception is the coin issue, but it is so tiny as hardly to matter nowadays. But see the discussion of the status of metallic money in Wicksell's monetary economics in the footnotes on p. 23 and p. 60.

the case. It seems to follow that deposits can be increased by the simultaneous addition of identical sums to both sides of a bank's balance sheet. The expansion of its balance sheet occurs if a bank sees a profitable opportunity to buy a security (when it credits a sum to the account of the person who sells the security and the security becomes part of its assets) or to make a new loan (when it credits a sum to the borrower's deposit, which is its liability, and registers the same sum on the assets side of the balance sheet as a loan). It is certainly the case that in modern circumstances much money creation does take place in this way, so that deposits have been described as 'fountain-pen money' (Pepper and Oliver 2006: 58), 'cheque-book money' ('check-book money' in American spelling; Barber 1997: 43–47) or 'keyboard money' to reflect the ever-evolving technology of writing.

But there is a catch. Commercial banks do not have the power to issue legal tender cash. Since they must at all times be able to convert customers' deposits back into central bank notes, they must keep a cash reserve (partly in their vaults and tills, and partly in a deposit at the central bank) to meet deposit withdrawals. If an individual bank expands its balance sheet too quickly relative to other banks, it may find its deposits have become so large that cash withdrawals exceed cash inflows. Potentially it could run out of cash. The expansion of deposits by commercial banks is therefore constrained by the imperative to maintain a positive cash reserve. Indeed, over multi-decadal periods in many nations commercial banks have kept a relatively stable ratio of cash to their deposit liabilities.

Two approaches

The discussion suggests two approaches to conceptualising the creation of money in a fiat-money economy. The creation of money can be seen, first, as the result of the extension of credit by the banking system, where the system is consolidated to embrace both the central bank and the commercial banks. The 'credit counterparts' on the assets side of the consolidated banking system's balance sheet must equal the liabilities on the other, and can be categorised in several ways. For example, assets could be viewed as the sum of loans, securities and cash. However, to split them into claims on the domestic private and public sectors, and the overseas sector, is more interesting, as private borrowers and the government have different motives when they seek bank finance. It is, of course, the deposit liabilities which are monetary in nature and so are of most significance to the subject in hand. Non-monetary liabilities include banks' equity capital plus their bond issues plus an assortment of odds and ends, such as deferred tax. Clearly, an identity can be stated:

> Change in the quantity of money (i.e. in bank deposits, and notes and coin in circulation) = Change in banking system assets – Change in its non-monetary liabilities;

and in more detail

> Change in the quantity of money = Change in banks' net claims on the public sector + Change in net claims on the

private sector + Change in banks' net claims on the overseas sector – Change in their non-monetary liabilities.

Central banks and the International Monetary Fund have large databases on the credit counterparts to money growth, and the information is basic to monetary analysis.[2]

The other approach to money creation takes its cue from banks' need to maintain cash reserves to honour obligations to customers (that is, obligations to repay deposits and to fulfil payment instructions). As has been noted, in some historical periods, banks have maintained stable ratios of cash to deposit liabilities. In their transactions, members of the non-bank public can use either cash or bank deposits, depending on their relative convenience and cost. If transactions technology is fairly stable, the ratio of the non-bank public's cash to its deposits ought also to change little over time. It follows that deposits held by the non-bank public can be viewed as a multiple of their cash holdings. Indeed, the quantity of money as a whole can be understood as a multiple of the total amount of cash issued by the central bank.[3]

The credit counterparts arithmetic and the base multiplier approach add value to thinking about the monetary situation, and no one can dispute that both are legitimate

---

[2] Perhaps the most important of the papers crucial to the development of credit counterparts analysis was written in the mid 1950s by the International Monetary Fund's second head of research, Jacques Polak (1957). See also Steel (2014).

[3] The derivation of the banking system multiplier is a textbook commonplace. But see, for example, Friedman and Schwartz (1963a: 776–808) for a rigorous treatment.

as accounting frameworks. In this book the preference is very much for the credit counterparts framework rather than that which appeals to the base multiplier. This preference would upset Milton Friedman, as is noted below in chapter 10. All the same, it is crucial to the sketches, in chapter 8 and 9, of the relationship between money and inflation in the US and the UK in the 2020s, and to the successful forecasts based on that relationship.

Money-issuers vs. money-holders

Evidently, a modern economy contains both money-holders and money-issuers. The money-holders include the non-bank private sector agents (households, companies and non-bank financial institutions) who or which typically carry out about 80% of the economy's expenditure and are the only net wealth-holders.[4] By contrast, the banking system is the dominant money-issuer. Banks specialise in carrying out payment instructions from their customers, a business in which they deploy distinctive expertise and have made large investments.

Of course, banks have to settle debts between themselves, which they do by means of transfers across central bank reserves. Such reserves, which are fully convertible into legal tender, do constitute 'money' for the banking industry, but only for it. Interbank settlement is largely for the purpose of matching up accounts and is purely financial in character. No goods and services, and no

---

4 The overwhelming majority of nations have positive net public debt.

payments for factors of production, are involved, and no effects on the expenditure–output flow or aggregate demand follow interbank settlement. Banks' cash reserves are therefore *not* part of the quantity of money. By extension, when banks hold balances with other banks, perhaps because of activity in an extensive interbank market, the resulting interbank deposits also do *not* belong to the quantity of money.[5]

One further participant in the economy is problematic from a monetary perspective: this is the state itself, and its constituent parts in central and local government. Because it has to protect a nation's borders against external

---

5 If a money demand function with the usual arguments (income and the own return on the deposits) were estimated for interbank deposits, the results would be worthless. However, a tricky definitional issue is raised. Non-bank financial institutions are of two kinds, those that receive deposits from customers and so have liabilities mostly fixed in nominal amounts, and those which have quite different liabilities and may even be managing assets with no fixed objective in mind. Those which take in deposits may not be legally the same as banks, but they are sufficiently similar as to be 'quasi-banks'. Should deposits at quasi-banks be included in money or not? For over 20 years the practice in the UK has been to measure deposits at quasi-banks when these come from banks and other quasi-banks, and to exclude such deposits from the true 'quantity of money'. The treatment is the same as with interbank deposits, with the definitionally inconvenient quasi-bank institutions known as 'intermediate other financial corporations'. Broad money in (what might be regarded as a legally complete definition) is called M4 and broad money excluding the IOFCs is M4x. M4x is the more appropriate definition of money in macroeconomic analysis. Similar difficulties are found in other countries, but the UK has taken a lead in separating out the IOFCs from the rest of the financial system. Notice that – again – estimating a conventional money demand function for IOFC deposits would be a silly exercise. To the extent that IOFC deposits are (unwisely) included in broad money, money demand functions are corrupted by their influence.

aggression and to enforce the law within those borders, the state has a monopoly of legitimate force in the kind of society under consideration.[6] It can therefore commandeer resources from citizens to an unlimited extent, at least in principle. Within its own borders its creditworthiness is unimpeachable; it does not need to hold significant money balances in order to be confident that 'it can pay its way'. Central and local governments do have accounts in the banking system, but the accounts are usually very small compared with incomings and outgoings; they are *not* included in the quantity of money. Public expenditure is neither constrained by nor systematically related to the state's money balances.[7] In short, the government's creditworthiness differs fundamentally from the private sector's.[8] This gives rise to crucial asymmetries which are sometimes neglected or not fully appreciated.[9]

---

6   The insight is usually attributed to Max Weber (2013) in his *Economy and Society*:

   A compulsory political organization with continuous operations will be called a 'state' [if and] insofar as its administrative staff successfully upholds a claim to the monopoly of the legitimate use of physical force in the enforcement of its order.

7   The point was noticed by the author in his first pamphlet on monetary economics (Congdon 1978: 56–58). The argument connected monetarism with the distinction between marketed (mostly private sector) output and non-marketed output (mostly public sector) in Bacon and Eltis (1976).

8   The euro zone is an unusual monetary jurisdiction, since governments cannot borrow without limit from the central bank. Discussion of this important point is beyond the scope of this book.

9   This may be the place to mention the so-called Hahn problem, advanced by the Cambridge economist Frank Hahn (1925–2013) in several papers. According to Hahn (1984: 261), 'the formulation of a model of the economy which can account for money is immensely difficult and remains to be

A logical point – often overlooked, but already adumbrated and essential to the larger argument – concludes this chapter. The quantity of money is held exclusively by genuinely non-bank private sector agents (households, companies, genuinely non-bank financial institutions) and cannot be changed by transactions between such agents. If purchases and sales between them take place in a closed circuit, these purchases and sales cannot alter the quantity of money. That is true, no matter how enormous the value of transactions. Alternatively put, in an economy with no external trade or financial flows with other economies, the quantity of money can change only as a result

---

accomplished.' See also chapter 7, 'On some problems of proving the existence of equilibrium in a monetary economy', in that book for more detail on the 'problem'. As this allegedly important issue was left unresolved, Hahn became a consistent critic of monetarism and Milton Friedman. With another Cambridge economist, Robert Neild, he organised a letter to *The Times* – signed by 364 British academic economists – in protest against the 1981 Budget, which had raised taxes in a recession in order to restore medium-term fiscal sustainability. For more on this episode, see essay 10 in Congdon (2011). Given the ubiquity of money use in modern market economies, and the evident massive saving of transactions costs relative to a barter-based economy arising from that, one has to ask whether Hahn intended his problem seriously. But the contrast between the private sector's and the state's creditworthiness may throw light on the matter. Private sector agents have finite creditworthiness and must therefore hold money in order to have the means to settle debts; the state has no such constraint and does not need to hold money for the same motive. An implication of this asymmetry is that, when money creation is financed by state borrowing from the banking system, the effect disrupts any pre-existing equilibrium in the private sector's balance sheet. Monetary policy – as traditionally understood – then becomes possible, rather obviously. Hahn is not the only academic to have put forward a seemingly fundamental conundrum of this sort. See the extensive discussion below in chapter 5 of the inside-money-is-not-net-wealth claim associated with names of Gurley and Shaw, and Patinkin.

of transactions between the non-bank private sector on the one hand, and the banking system and the state sector on the other.[10] This property of a monetary economy results from definitions and is beyond dispute. Nevertheless, the implications – which are a major undercurrent in the stream of analysis on the transmission mechanism in chapters 5 and 6 – turn out to be profound.

---

[10] The point is captured in the credit counterparts identity, as it is usually stated. The assumption of a closed economy is needed to keep the size of the discussion under control. The monetary approach to the balance of payments is a vast subject in its own right. The cogency of this approach depends on the possibility that excess or deficient money balances are removed by transactions with foreigners.

4 THE MONETARY THEORY OF NATIONAL INCOME AND WEALTH

The $MV = PT$ approach to the quantity theory – as expounded by the Yale of the early twentieth century, and the Chicago of the 1950s and 1960s – was shown in the second chapter to have serious drawbacks. Is there an alternative? One option is to pay more attention to the Cambridge, England, of the 1920s and 1930s, where Keynes was interacting with colleagues and rivals, and they together constituted 'the Cambridge School' of monetary economics. Their inspiration came significantly from Alfred Marshall, who had founded the Cambridge economics faculty in 1903. A basic principle of Marshall's economics was that equilibrium – in terms of prices and quantities – was reached when supply equalled demand. The principle conquered the teaching of microeconomics from that time onwards. But Marshall wanted to use it not only in understanding an individual's attitude towards his or her money holdings; he hoped also that it might help in expounding the relationship – for the economy as a whole – between the total amount of money on the one hand, and income and 'property' on the other (Marshall 1922, quoted in Keynes 1971: 229–30; see also Walters 1971: 28–34). In the 1930 *Treatise on Money* Keynes lifted an entire passage from Marshall's 1922 *Money, Credit and Commerce*, which ran as follows:

> In every state of society there is some fraction of their income which people find it worth while to hold in the form of currency ... Let us suppose that the inhabitants of a country ... find it just worth their while [after judging the advantages and disadvantages of holding currency] to keep by them on the average ready purchasing power to the extent of a tenth part of their annual income, together with a fiftieth part of their property; then the aggregate value of the currency of the country will tend to be equal to the sum of these amounts.

In the related footnote, Keynes (1971: 230, footnote 1) commented:

> In modern conditions the normal proportion ... of ... total [bank] deposits to the national income seems to be somewhere around a half.

He was writing in the late 1920s. Over 30 years later in the first quarter of 1964, when the Bank of England had just started to prepare modern money supply statistics, the UK's nominal GDP was £32.6 billion and broad money, including building society deposits as well as bank deposits, was £15.0 billion. The ratio was still 'somewhere around a half'. (But note that the ratio was to rise steeply from 1980. It is not one of the constants of nature, a point which is recognised below in, for example, chapter 7.)

Money held in wealth portfolios

Marshall's teaching motivated similar treatments, of his so-called cash balance approach, in the early-twentieth-century literature. An ambitious statement of the meaning of these ideas for macroeconomics follows at the end of the section, but attention needs to be paid first to certain key facts about present-day economies. It is important to recognise that money is held not only to facilitate transactions in capital and current items in the income–expenditure–output flow, but also to reside over long periods in investment portfolios as an alternative to non-money assets. Marshall had of course seen this with his reference to 'property' in the above quotation. What is to be said about 'property' in the real world, about the value and composition of household wealth?

Table 2 presents the relevant data for the US at the end of 2021. Money was then about 11% of gross household wealth, and was exceeded in importance only by corporate equities and real estate (mostly houses of course), which both represented over a quarter of such wealth, and by life insurance policies and claims on pension funds, which were a fifth.[1] The bulk of corporate equities were quoted on the US's stock markets. These compositional data suggest that, in a modern economy, the management of money in investment portfolios is to a considerable extent about seeking a balance between the 'liquidity' conferred by money, and the returns derived from housing, equities, savings products

---

1   Gross household wealth is wealth before the deduction of liabilities, that is, net wealth plus all debt.

managed by specialist financial institutions and other asset categories. The word 'liquidity' is an awkward one to define, but a basic theme is that assets which possess the property of liquidity reduce the expected future costs of running portfolios. Invariably, money offers a lower explicit return than non-money assets. Indeed, as has been noted, many money balances – like most sight deposits and current accounts – offer no nominal return at all.

Table 2   Value and composition of US household wealth at the end of 2021

	In $ billions	As % of total before debt
Money, mostly deposits	18,272	10.9
Debt securities	2,720	1.6
Corporate equities	44,723	26.6
Life and pension assets	33,623	20.0
Non-corporate equity	15,320	9.1
Other financial assets	3,064	1.8
Real estate, mostly houses	42,429	25.2
Consumer durables	7,286	4.3
Non-profit business assets	739	0.4
Total assets, before debt	168,177	100.0
Total liabilities	18,354	
Total assets, after debt	149,823	

Personal disposable income in 2021 was $18,507.6 billion.

In the US flow-of-funds data, non-profit organisations are presented with households, so that the above numbers include non-profit assets and debt, as well as households'.

Source: US Federal Reserve *Financial Accounts of the United States* (June 2023 release), Table B101, p. 154.

The important notion of 'liquidity'

But money is retained in investment portfolios, even when these are seeking significant positive returns, because a money holding lowers the cost of rearranging portfolios and taking advantage of opportunities. In practice, different people have different preferences and investment habits. In his last book, on *The Market Theory of Money*, the influential English economist and Nobel laureate, Sir John Hicks (1904–89) – who has already been mentioned in the introduction – suggested a new nomenclature. He said that some investors (whom he called 'fluid') might want to hold a high ratio of money to assets in order to actively exploit opportunities, whereas others might be 'solid' investors. Solid investors would hold little money and stick to the securities they had first chosen (Hicks 1989: 67). More generally, portfolios can be said to have different degrees of 'liquidity', as well as the better-known characteristics of expected mean return and the risks associated with earning that return. However difficult to formalise and quantify, liquidity is an attribute of asset portfolios.

Table 2 shows that directly held debt securities – or 'bonds', more concisely – were a mere 1.6% of gross US household wealth at the end of 2021. By implication, a great majority of households – accounting for the distribution of American wealth – did not have a single bond in their possession. Nevertheless, many economics textbooks give pride of place to bonds in their analyses of the alternatives to money in portfolios. The focus on the money-bond choice is conceptually claustrophobic, but it is entrenched in standard textbooks. This entrenchment has led to serious misunderstandings about how changes in the quantity of money affect the economy, as was noticed in the introduction and is discussed in more depth in chapter 6.

The 'identification problem'

Before finishing this chapter, a warning has to be given that the whole subject is bedevilled by what economists call 'an identification problem'. Marshall taught that, in equilibrium, the demand curve for a product intersects with the supply curve to determine both its price and quantity. But do the prices and quantities reported from a real-world situation signal the immaculate and pleasingly automatic meeting of supply and demand curves? Or do they instead reflect agents' confused attempts to interpret market data when no one knows the exact positions of the demand and supply curves? One point has been much emphasised in this book: it must be the case that the money held in an economy by various people and companies is equal to the actual quantity of money in being. But that definitional certainty misses a vital aspect. Is this equivalence also a position *of equilibrium*, analogous to that connoted by the intersection of supply and demand curves in a price–quantity diagram?

It may be that, at the end of a period of production and trading, people and companies find – for whatever reason – that their bank balances are not at the levels they expected and planned at the period's start. Money is then in disequilibrium. So in the following period these people and companies set different prices and quantities from before. More generally, the world is such a complicated place that it contains phases when the economy is at or near monetary equilibrium (that is, when the prices and quantities involved in determining national income show little tendency to change between periods) and phases of monetary disequilibrium (when those prices and quantities are changing constantly and perhaps dramatically between periods, and so are national expenditure, income and wealth).

Key statements: but is disequilibrium prevalent?

Enough disclaimers, caveats and qualifications have now been offered. Having distinguished between monetary equilibrium and disequilibrium, we have reached a decisive moment. The crux of the monetary theory of national income and wealth determination – as understood in the present study – can now be stated. Here it is, indented because of its significance to our argument.

> The level of expenditure *by genuinely non-bank private sector agents* and the value of all the assets they own (their wealth) are in equilibrium, and in that sense determined, only when the broadly defined quantity of money is willingly held – at the associated prices and quantities – by the same private sector agents.

This way of expressing the quantity theory notices the nuisance caused by *the state's* attitude towards money, since an expansion in aggregate demand due to more government spending may have a small or unclear effect on *the private sector's* demand to hold money.[2] Let this complication be ignored, with the balance between public and private economic activity taken to be fixed. We reach the following core proposition, in the spirit of the inter-war Cambridge School:

> The *equilibrium* levels of national income and wealth reflect the interaction of two influences:
> - the level of the broadly defined money aggregate, as determined by the banking system, its customers and monetary policymakers, and
> - the ratio of money to national income *desired* by money holders, where the relevant money holders are genuine non-bank private sector agents (households; companies; non-bank, non-deposit-taking financial institutions) who or which have a meaningful 'money demand function'.

The proposition overcomes the criticisms of the 'hotchpotch' price index implied by the transactions version of the equation of exchange, and of the question-begging, unsatisfactory phrase 'the income velocity of circulation' implied by its income version; it is precise about the concept

---

2 Before the privatisations of the 1980s and early 1990s, UK public corporations had an account at the Treasury, a government department, and typically only minor bank accounts; after privatisation they all had bank accounts, sometimes large ones. Privatisation therefore raised the equilibrium ratio of money to GDP.

of money relevant to national income determination, and about the agents who or which matter to the economy's monetary equilibrium; and it makes room for those sceptical about monetarism by acknowledging that in the real world, monetary equilibrium does not hold all the time. Admittedly, the words 'equilibrium' and 'desired' carry much weight in the proposition just stated. Further, a related and perhaps major concession has been made by admitting the possible prevalence of monetary disequilibrium.[3]

---

[3] The argument here emphasises that the key quantity-theory propositions are valid only in equilibrium. This emphasis on their equilibrium character of the propositions is not new. It was noticed, for example, by Schumpeter in his *History of Economic Analysis* (Schumpeter (1981: 1102). To illustrate, after the 19% jump in M3 in the mere five months to July 2020, the US economy was plainly not in equilibrium. Only in coming quarters and years would money-holders take steps to restore equilibrium, and the resulting processes of adjustment would cause a significant rise in the price level. See chapter 8 for further discussion.

5 THE TRANSMISSION MECHANISM: DIRECT EFFECTS IN 'THE GOODS MARKET'[1]

Complaints are sometimes made that the quantity theory is vague about how the economy moves towards and achieves a new equilibrium when a shock change to the quantity of money has occurred. Paul Samuelson (1915–2009), a Nobel laureate and long-time rival of Milton Friedman, once asserted that the vagueness went so far as to make the so-called 'transmission mechanism' of monetary change 'a black box'. In his view monetarism sometimes came in 'garden-variety' form, when it was 'a black-box theory' with 'mechanistic regularities' which could not be 'spelled out by any plausible economic theory' (Samuelson 1972: 755).

---

[1] Textbooks refer to 'the goods market', the market in currently produced goods and services relevant to the determination of national income and expenditure, to distinguish it from the markets in assets. Asset transactions may have profound implications for expenditure in the goods market, but, strictly speaking, they do not take place 'in the goods market' and are not part of it. The related distinction between the direct and indirect effects in the transmission mechanism – used here to organise the discussion in chapters 5 and 6 – is owed to Blaug (1985), particularly chapters 5 and 15.

The black-box allegation

Similar allegations continue to be made. In a speech in Glasgow on 4 April 2023, Silvana Tenreyro, while serving the final months of her term as an external member of the Bank of England's Monetary Policy Committee, said that the effects of monetary policy were felt throughout the economy solely via interest rates and bond yields. She saw it as her job (Tenreyro 2023)

> to make clearer the similarities between [central bank operations meant to affect bond yields, but which might increase the quantity of money] and Bank Rate, and avoid the impression that there is an independent 'money' channel of [such operations].

Here was interest-rate-only macroeconomics at its most explicit and brazen. In making this claim Tenreyro reflected the influence of Michael Woodford of Columbia University, New York, the author of a 2003 work entitled *Interest and Prices: Foundations of a Theory of Monetary Policy*. According to Woodford (2003: 109), 'a straightforward analysis ... of inflation ... is possible without any reference to either the evolution of the money supply or the determinants of money demand.'

In fact, accounts of the transmission mechanism – and hence of 'an independent "money" channel' – have abounded in a large and classic literature since David Hume and Richard Cantillon in the eighteenth century. One of the most lucid was given by Knut Wicksell

(1851–1926), the Swedish economist, in his 1898 work, *Geldzins und Güterpreise*, translated into English and published under the auspices of the Royal Economic Society in 1936 as *Interest and Prices: A Study of the Causes Regulating the Value of Money*.[2] The key passage begins with the situation termed in the present work 'a monetary equilibrium'. In this situation the amount of money held by all individuals – including 'myself' – is appropriate given incomes and expenditure, and the associated price level of goods and services. But a shock is delivered. To quote from the 1936 translation:

> Now let us suppose that for some reason or other commodity prices rise while the stock of money remains unchanged, or that the stock of money is diminished while prices remain temporarily unchanged. The cash balances will gradually appear to be too small in relation to the new level of prices ... I therefore seek to enlarge my balance. This can only be done – neglecting for the present the possibility of borrowing etc. – through a reduction in my demand for goods and services, or through an increase in [the supply of] my own commodity, or through both together. The same is true of all other owners and consumers of commodities ... But in fact no one will succeed in realising the object at which each is aiming – to

---

2   The 2003 Woodford book has the same title as Wicksell's 1898 contribution, with Woodford claiming to write in a 'neo-Wicksellian' tradition. But the subtitles of the two books are very different, and some might feel – with the author – that the agenda and emphases of the two books are also very different.

increase his cash balance, for the sum of the individual cash balances is limited by the amount of the available stock of money, or rather is identical with it. On the other hand, the universal reduction in demand and increase in the supply of commodities will necessarily bring about a continuous fall in all prices. This can only cease when prices have fallen to a level at which the cash balances are regarded as adequate.

Many subsequent accounts of the transmission mechanism are in a similar vein. Important examples were provided in Irving Fisher's *Elementary Principles of Economics* and Keynes's *Treatise on Money*.[3] In 1959 Friedman prepared a statement to the US Congress which recalled Wicksell's themes (Friedman 1959: 141). When individuals have an excess holding of money, they cannot rid themselves of the excess by transactions between themselves. In that event, according to Friedman, 'they would simply be playing a

---

3 For the background to Fisher's treatment in his *Elementary Principles*, see Congdon (2005: 23–24). Keynes's treatment of the demand for real balances in chapter 14 of the *Treatise* was very much in the quantity-theoretic tradition (see especially Keynes 1971: 199–205). Typically, these discussions are about the sequel to a change in the level of the quantity of money. When commentators have to respond to the flow of real-world events, usually a change in the rate of growth of money is the focus of attention. Only two theoretical treatments are known to the author which discuss the sequel to a change in the rate of growth of money. The first was prepared by Milton Friedman and Anna Schwartz as they came towards the end of the work which led to their 1963 *Monetary History*. See the pages about 'the tentative sketch' in Friedman and Schwartz (1963b). The other was written by the author after he had successfully forecast in the late 1980s than an acceleration in broad money growth in the UK would result in an acceleration in inflation (Congdon 1992: 171–90).

game of musical chairs'.[4] In response to a sudden increase in the quantity of money, expenditure decisions would keep on being revised – with new prices and quantities – until the right balance between money and incomes had been restored. While individuals may be, to quote Friedman,

> frustrated in their attempt to reduce the number of dollars they hold, they succeed in achieving the equivalent change in their position, for the rise in money income and in prices reduces the ratio of these balances to their income and also the real value of these balances.

These excerpts from Wicksell and Friedman call for elucidation. Four points will be developed in this chapter to elaborate key ideas. But the incorporation of wealth and asset prices in the transmission mechanism has such far-reaching ramifications that it demands a chapter – the next chapter, chapter 6 – to itself.

Prices respond to change in money

First, in Wicksell's account a rise in the price level, or a fall in the quantity of money, is posited at the start. This

---

4 James Tobin used the analogy of a 'hot potato' in his account of the matter, rather than Friedman's 'musical chairs' (Tobin 1971: 273):

> [I]t is the beginning of wisdom in monetary economics to observe that money is like the 'hot potato' in a children's game: one individual may pass it to another, but the group as a whole cannot get rid of it.

The sentence appeared originally in a 1963 article on 'Commercial banks as creators of money'.

creates a disequilibrium. In his words, the quantity of money is 'too small' relative to the price level. The key agents – the 'owners and consumers of commodities' – are motivated in their behaviour by the disequilibrium, the difference between the quantity of money appropriate to the price level and the actual quantity of money. They spend less, leading to 'a universal reduction in demand'.

This is all plain and straightforward, or so one would have thought. Friedman hoped that even members of Congress would appreciate the force of the argument. On what basis can the past few sentences be characterised as being about 'a black box'? The words are about as clear and transparent as they could be in the sometimes arcane subject of economics. Further, Wicksell's 'universal reduction in demand' arises from the gap between agents' money holdings and the desired amount of these holdings, and nothing else. Contrary to Tenreyro's April 2023 speech, it does *not* arise from 'the rate of interest', whether that be the central bank rate, a bond yield, the interbank rate or banks' loan rate. It also does *not* arise from 'credit conditions', 'credit spreads' or the quantity of new bank loans to the private sector. Sure enough, 'the rate of interest' (in one or many of its multiple meanings), 'credit conditions', 'credit spreads' and new bank credit are relevant to the description of full monetary equilibrium, and to the transition from one equilibrium to another. But first things must come first, and all of the list in the last two sentences are secondary or tertiary relative to money-holders' attitudes and intentions.

The proportionality postulate

The second issue arising from the Wicksell and Friedman passages is the extent to which prices change because of the shock to the quantity of money. Wicksell said that, in the monetary disequilibrium under discussion, agents' transactions continue to affect the price level until money balances are again 'adequate', again – that is – in equilibrium with agents' money-holding preferences. How much does the change in prices need to be? In *Interest and Prices* Wicksell expressed doubts about the quantity theory's boldest claim in this area of economics, that changes in money and the price level would – in the real world – be proportional much of the time.[5] But he did mention respectfully John Stuart Mill (1806–73), the British economist whose *Principles of Political Economy* was the standard textbook of the late nineteenth century. As Wicksell quoted from Mill's *Principles*, he would undoubtedly have been aware of chapter VIII of its book III, entitled 'Of the value of money, as dependent on supply and demand'. A crucial section ran (Mill 1900: 298–99):

---

5 By 'money' Wicksell understood only 'metallic money'. At the time he was writing this was not a silly assumption, but it was being rapidly outdated by the growth of banking. Much of the argument of *Interest and Prices* is in fact about the alleged supersession of the quantity theory of money in a world where payments were increasingly being made from bank deposits created by the extension of bank credit. Wicksell did not make the leap of regarding bank deposits as money. For the tendency of his contemporaries to describe 'bank deposits' (that is, money to modern economists) as 'credit', see Laidler's (1991) treatment, particularly pp. 14–15.

> The value or purchasing power of money depends ... on supply and demand ... The supply of money ... is the quantity of it which people want to lay out ... [It], in short, is the money *in circulation* at the time ... Supposing the quantity of money in the hands of individuals to be increased, the wants and inclinations of the community collectively in respect to consumption remaining exactly the same; the increase in demand would reach all things equally, and there would be a universal rise of prices ... Prices would have risen in a certain proportion, and the value of money would have fallen in the same ratio ... If the whole money in circulation was doubled, prices would be doubled.[6]

Thus, a doubling of the quantity of money leads to a doubling of the price level.[7] The argument – sometimes called 'the proportionality postulate' (or 'proportionality hypothesis') – can be translated into more modern language, and remains central to contemporary economics. Given the economy's supply-side characteristics, and assuming stability in agents' demand-to-hold-money function and no changes to the arguments in that function (apart from the quantity of money itself), changes in the quantity of money and the price level are equi-proportional in equilibrium. To be clear, this is *not* an assertion that changes in the quantity of money and the price level are

---

6 Later in his *Principles* Mill qualified this conclusion by again – as with Wicksell a few decades later – invoking 'credit'.

7 David Hume made the same argument over a century earlier (Mayer 1980: 89–101).

always equi-proportional in actual experience. However, the proportionality postulate still lies at the heart of quantity-theoretic doctrine, even if nowadays proportionality is usually understood to hold between money and national income rather than money and the price level.

Inside money vs. outside money

The argument in this restatement of the quantity theory has been that a broadly defined, all-inclusive measure of money is appropriate for macroeconomic analysis. It is important now, in a third area of discussion prompted by the quotations from Wicksell and Friedman, to anticipate and refute a sophisticated objection which is sometimes made. Crucial to our argument has been the idea that – once the quantity of money has been determined – transactions between money-holders cannot change it. In a 1956 classic work on *Money, Income and Prices* Donald Patinkin (1922–95) put forward a terminology to elaborate the ideas and their implications.

He called the attempts by particular isolated agents to change their money balances 'individual experiments'. Individual experiments may alter the amounts that each agent holds and the distribution of money between agents. But – assuming that transactions take place within a closed circuit – they do not change the total quantity of money. Patinkin's phrase for changes in the total quantity of money was 'the market experiment'. Much of his book was about how, because of the underlying stability of agents' demand to hold *real* money balances, changes in the *nominal* aggregate quantity of money would ultimately affect nothing real and result merely in the same proportionate change in the price level. He emphasised that a 'real balance effect' ensured an eventual alignment between money and prices.[8]

A challenge to Patinkin came in a 1960 volume *Money in a Theory of Finance* by John Gurley (1920–2020) and Edward Shaw (1908–94), which Patinkin himself described – in a 1965 second edition of *Money, Interest and Prices* – as 'pathbreaking' (Patinkin 1965: 295). The Gurley and Shaw book recalled that the quantity of money contained notes in circulation with the public, a liability of the central bank, and bank deposits, which are liabilities of commercial banks; they labelled that part of money issued by the central bank 'outside money' and that part issued by commercial banks 'inside money'; and they further remembered that the non-bank private sector both kept deposits with the commercial banks and borrowed from it. By implication, an increase in inside money, or bank deposits, due to a rise in bank borrowing from the private sector could not alter the net wealth of the non-bank private sector. Patinkin, along with Gurley, Shaw and others, further reasoned that – because this type of money expansion could not affect net wealth – it could not affect anything. Patinkin went so far as to say that enquiries into the effects of changes in inside money (that is, bank deposits) were 'meaningless'

---

8   The phrase 'real balances' seems to have been used first by Keynes (1972: 192, footnote 2).

(Patinkin 1965: 300).[9] In his view, the real balance effect related to outside money (the monetary base, more or less) and only to outside money, and that was that.[10]

If the Gurley and Shaw objection to inside money were persuasive, and if Patinkin's endorsement of it were correct, the present exercise in broad-money monetarism would be

---

9   The Chicago-based Nobel laureate, Eugene Fama (1980), also went down this track. He agreed with Patinkin, and Gurley and Shaw, that – as inside money growth does not constitute a positive wealth effect – it cannot affect anything. All these authors seem to have overlooked that, if this argument can be made about commercial banks' liabilities, it can also be made about the central bank's liabilities ('outside money'). The reasoning is straightforward. If central banks' assets are entirely claims on the private sector (such as the mortgage-backed securities now held in large amounts by the Federal Reserve) and central bank liabilities are also held 100% by the private sector, the private sector cannot be better off if the central bank expands. The situation might appear more promising if central bank assets are claims on government. But – if Barro's (1974) contention that public debt is not net wealth in the hands of the public is accepted – then again, an increase in the monetary base as a result of central bank acquisition of government debt is not a positive wealth effect. In short, if the thesis of Fama's 1980 article were right, monetary policy – understood as the consequences of changes in the balance sheets of either the central bank or the commercial banks – could not affect anything. 'Fama's attack on the problem of integrating monetary theory and value theory is radical: he simply abolishes monetary theory' (Hoover 1988: 5). The conclusion is peculiar, even nonsensical. Evidently, something has gone wrong. Might one suggest that an increase in the quantity of money influences the economy by a mechanism other than a wealth effect? Perhaps it does so – as suggested in this chapter – by changing the liquidity of the non-bank private sector. In an interview for a *New Yorker* journalist in 2009, when asked about the causes of the then Great Recession, Fama replied, 'We don't know what causes recessions … We've never known' (Mirowski 2013: 179).

10 In other words, Patinkin approved of what might be termed 'monetary-base monetarism'. For more on this approach, see the remarks about it in the introduction and the author's 2023 paper on the subject (Congdon 2023b). In the author's view the approach disintegrates when confronted with obvious facts about real-world institutions and magnitudes.

misconceived from top to bottom. However, these authors' critique of inside money is questionable and arguably quite wrong. The misunderstandings are two-fold. First, Patinkin wrote as if the private sector were one agent. But of course, it consists of millions of people and companies, and they have different preferences and capabilities. (If the private sector were one agent, there would, in any case, be no point in that agent borrowing from itself.) The agents who or which hold money are not the same as the agents who or which borrow from banks, while the existence of a banking sector modifies the economy's production possibilities and the scope for intertemporal substitution. Changes in the size of bank deposits are not neutral and self-cancelling in their effects on the non-bank private sector, in part because it contains a multiplicity of heterogeneous agents.[11]

Second, and even more fundamentally, banks engage in so-called liquidity transformation. They invest in payments infrastructure, and offer money transmission and settlement services to their customers. As the costs of using deposits to make payments are therefore very low, the deposit liabilities on one side of the banking system balance sheet are highly liquid to private sector non-bank agents (households, companies and so on). On the other hand, the costs of taking out a bank loan include negotiation and the offering of collateral, while the bank has the costs of attracting and sustaining its funding of the loan.

---

[11] If changes in the size of bank balance sheets cannot affect anything, one has to wonder why banks exist at all.

The assets side of the banking system balance sheet is illiquid to private sector non-banks. An increase in inside money may not in the first instance add to net wealth, but it does alter the non-bank private sector's liquidity. We must remember Hicks's insistence that liquidity is an attribute of portfolios.[12] One side of banks' balance sheets can be viewed as portfolios of assets and the other as portfolios of liabilities.

Because of its importance, the argument needs more detail. All companies are legal fictions, in the sense that balance sheets balance, and assets and liabilities are the same. But in modern conditions companies are the dominant agents taking decisions on non-housing capital expenditure and inventory accumulation, with major repercussion on aggregate demand, output and employment. Their balance sheets have a mixture of liquid assets (particularly, their money holdings) and illiquid assets (notably such items as 'goodwill', which are notoriously difficult to value). If a particular concern has a high ratio of liquid to illiquid assets, this indicates that it has less vulnerability to cash-flow shocks than one with a low ratio. Stakeholders and analysts can therefore talk about the 'strength' or 'weakness' of corporate balance sheets,

---

[12] Stracca (2007) regards inside money as 'money produced by the private sector', although how money-holders are to know whether the money they receive from a particular transaction has this property is unclear. Bank deposits are said to help in 'alleviating asymmetric information between buyers and sellers'. Stracca exemplifies the belief among central bank economists that the inside-money-is-not-net-wealth argument is cogent and important.

and expect such strength and weakness to affect corporate decisions.[13]

As changes in inside money have an impact on the liquidity of company balance sheets, they are also very relevant to demand, output and employment. In short, the *ratios* between different components of corporate balance sheets can be of immense significance to macroeconomic outcomes, even if the *levels* of assets and liabilities – for both banks and non-bank companies – are always identical. Famously, Karl Marx believed that double-entry book-keeping was crucial to the emergence of capitalism. Organisations with balance sheets are of course very much the norm in the corporate sectors of today's advanced capitalist societies. Economists must be barking up the wrong tree if a branch of their subject contends that such organisations can be eliminated from its analytical purview, effectively by assumption.

Anyhow, the empirical evidence is overwhelming that changes in bank deposits – in 'inside money' – have powerful macroeconomic effects. (See chapter 7 below on the facts.) If Patinkin, Gurley, Shaw and their followers were correct, annual growth rates of inside money of 20% or 200% or 2,000% would be associated with identical

---

13 When in early 2009 making the case for (the operations which became) the UK's 'quantitative easing' programme, the author estimated an equation for the relationship between, as the independent variable, the company sector's ratio of bank deposits to its bank borrowing, and, as the dependent variable, the growth rate of real private domestic demand. The equation had explanatory power, while the t statistic on the independent variable met the usual statistical test (Congdon 2009: 4–5).

macroeconomic outcomes because the two sides of the banking system balance sheet cancel out and changes in the size of the balance sheet are 'a wash'.[14] This is clearly very far from reality.[15]

Is bank credit so special?

One further topic needs clarification. Wicksell inserted a phrase – 'neglecting the possibility of borrowing' – to qualify his claim that a deficiency of money balances would result in a 'universal reduction in demand'. This was remarkably prescient, in that it anticipated a much later major debate in monetary economics. Wicksell realised that the deficiency of money balances could be eliminated not by non-bank agents' attempts to acquire more money by spending less, but by some of these agents borrowing from the banks and thereby creating more money. In exchanges with Friedman over 70 years later,

---

14 Today's central bankers occasionally appeal to the inside-money-is-not-net-wealth argument. In a speech in April 2023 Ben Broadbent, deputy governor of the Bank of England, remarked, 'at least for the private sector as a whole, its interactions with the banking system – deposit claims on the one hand, bank loans on the other – are essentially a wash and do not represent net wealth' (Broadbent 2023).

15 The statistical database maintained for over 60 years by the International Monetary Fund for its scores of members relates to the credit counterparts to broad money growth. The analytical framework is designed to inform the agenda for countries with a need to repay foreign borrowings. If the banking system's balance sheet were merely 'a wash', the IMF approach – used, for example, in setting IMF programmes for the UK in the late 1960s and 1970s – would be misconceived. The growth rate of bank lending to the private sector could reach any number – a number into the hundreds per cent – and not matter for anything.

the Cambridge economist Nicholas Kaldor (1908–86) correctly saw that this meant that an economy with fiat money could behave differently from an economy with commodity money.

He then leapt to an extraordinary conclusion, that an excess or deficiency of money balances would *always* be brought to an end by changes in bank borrowing. Suppose that gold has ceased to be money and all money is the result of bank credit extension. Then, to quote from Kaldor's 1981 Radcliffe lectures at the University of Warwick, reprinted in a 1982 pamphlet entitled *The Scourge of Monetarism* (Kaldor 1982: 22):

> If ... more money comes into existence than the public, at a given or expected level of incomes or expenditures, wishes to hold, the excess will be automatically *extinguished* – either through debt repayment or its conversion into interest-bearing assets.[16]

According to Kaldor, an excess or deficiency of money could therefore never motivate changes in expenditure or investment portfolios, as our excerpts from Wicksell and Friedman have argued.

But Kaldor's objection to monetarism is utterly implausible, because of the relative size in any economy of the change in bank borrowing and the level of total

---

[16] Kaldor's italics are in the original. His statement is correct only if the repayment is of bank debt or if 'the interest-bearing assets' are acquired from the banking system. Why the debt repayment or asset acquisition should always and automatically take this form is unclear and not explained.

transactions. The common pattern is for new bank credit to be less than one quarter of 1% of the value of transactions. This fact should be sufficient to demolish the notion that new bank credit would quickly and automatically, as a matter of routine, ensure that the demand to hold money was aligned with the actual quantity of money. Moreover, the value of transactions – which is of course equal to the quantity of money multiplied by its transactions velocity – is always positive. Indeed, it must be positive whether the stock of bank credit is rising, stable or falling.

Despite these problems, Kaldor's polemics encouraged a school of thought which emphasised that much money creation is the result of what were termed 'endogenous' processes. These were processes in which private sector agents interacted with each other in the creation or destruction of money balances, and did so independently of the state and the central bank. Many of its supporters went further by claiming that nominal national income and expenditure determined the quantity of money, rather than the other way round. In this cameo of so-called reverse causation, Wicksell's 'possibility of borrowing' was the usual mechanism to which they appealed.

The literature is extensive, but a few brief empirical observations should be enough to cast doubt on the most extreme claims from the endogenous money school. The heart of this school's approach is that, because banks' customers can borrow or repay loans from the banks, national income determines the quantity of money. But the great majority of bank loans are extended to acquire existing assets, meaning assets which were made in the past.[17] Such loan transactions are part of Keynes's 'financial circulation'. *They have no necessary connection with current national income and expenditure, and no first-round effect on the income–expenditure flow.* In this sense they do not properly belong to a discussion concerned with the setting of national income or expenditure at all.[18]

It must again be reiterated and emphasised that new bank credit is less than one quarter of 1% of the value of transactions. Bluntly and obviously, the value of transactions – and the associated values of national income and expenditure – cannot be explained by new bank lending alone. Some American economists have proposed that 'the credit channel' – with a focus on the 'special nature' of bank credit – is crucial to the transmission mechanism of monetary policy.[19] One motive of the credit channel idea seems to be to contrast 'creditism' and 'monetarism', and to put a credit-based account of national income on

---

17 A high proportion – often over a half – of banks' claims on the private sector are residential mortgages. A standard pattern in most economies is that the number of mortgages extended, in any period, is a multiple of new houses built for purchase in the private sector.

18 Let it be conceded bank credit can affect spending and output when second- or third-round effects are introduced. In the first round a bank creates new money by extending a loan to buy an asset, with the asset taken as loan collateral; in the second round the new money may be used in the purchase of goods and services; and so on. But – rather obviously – in this example the second-round transaction is subordinate to the monetary theory of national income determination. Bank credit matters because it creates money; it does not matter – or at any rate it does not matter much – to national income determination in its own right.

19 The 'credit channel' of monetary policy transmission has been proposed by, for example, Bernanke and Blinder (1988) and Bernanke and Gertler (1995).

a pedestal high enough that it rivals or even overshadows a money-based account. Given the quantitative insignificance of new bank credit and the preponderance of asset transfers as the first-round motive of bank credit extension, this is surely untenable.[20]

Indeed, another knockdown argument is available. Many agents have no bank debt whatsoever, but they engage in spending and investing, and so participate in the determination of national income and wealth. If they have no bank borrowings, how can bank credit be relevant to their expenditure and portfolio decisions? Of course, in a modern economy with no barter, every agent must have money to enter into transactions with other agents. Relative to the ubiquity of money, and transactions involving the use of money, credit-linked transactions are rare.[21] Purely credit-based accounts of national income determination are mistakes.

---

[20] Ben Bernanke was nevertheless awarded the Nobel prize in 2022 for his work on bank credit. See the Nobel Prize lecture 'Banking, credit and economic fluctuations' (https://www.nobelprize.org/prizes/economic-sciences/2022/bernanke/lecture/).

[21] Credit card payment may seem to be an exception to this remark. But most credit card accounts are linked to bank accounts and credit cards are not money. Correctly, changes in the amounts owed on credit cards have never been regarded as of any macroeconomic importance.

6 THE TRANSMISSION MECHANISM: INDIRECT EFFECTS VIA ASSET MARKETS

So far, the discussion of the passages from Wicksell and Friedman has adhered to their way of seeing equilibration as between money and 'commodities', or money and 'goods and services'. This has the merit of clarity, of arriving at the heart of the matter without too much fuss. However, it is misleading. In the real world, agents have to judge the right level of their money balances also against their payments to factors of production, and – much more importantly – against assets in their investment portfolios. In practice, the reaction of non-money assets to changes in the quantity of money has been one of the most vexed and unsettled areas of monetary economics. Table 2 showed that in the US, the main non-money assets are housing and corporate equity, which, taken together, are worth almost 5 times as much as money in household wealth, and 40 times as much as bonds. Although every economy has its own capital market structures and tax systems, similar patterns are found in all the world's capitalist liberal democracies.

Variable-income assets vs. fixed-income assets

In these societies, wealth is dominated by assets where the income they generate rises or falls over time, in line with cyclical fluctuations in national income and output. Such assets can be termed 'variable-income assets'. Happily, economic growth has ensured that the long-run trend has been for the nominal incomes from assets to increase. On the other hand, bonds are 'fixed-income assets'. As already noticed, one message of Table 2 was that very few households own fixed-income assets directly.

But households do own such products as life insurance policies, with a high proportion of bonds in their assets, and mutual funds invested 100% in bonds. At the end of 2021 the total assets of non-financial corporate businesses in the US were estimated to have been almost $57,000 billion, with the bulk of this (almost $33,000 billion) belonging to shareholders. Non-equity liabilities of $24,167.4 billion included liabilities in the form of debt securities amounting to $7,489.4 billion.[1] Moreover, government debt – at the end of 2021 over 120% of GDP in gross terms – was predominantly of fixed-interest securities. Roughly speaking, the value of bonds traded in the

---

[1] At the end of 2021 the market value of corporate equities, including unquoted equities, was $51,341.2 billion, according to the Federal Reserve. The market value of equities was well above the book value in company accounts. At the same date the Federal Reserve estimated the assets of non-financial non-corporate business – including unincorporated, mostly quite small businesses – as almost $26,000 billion, with liabilities of just above $10,000 billion. According to the Fed data, non-corporate business had issued no debt securities at all (Federal Reserve 2023: 139–40).

US is (at the time of writing, March 2024) about twice the value of GDP.

Bonds are therefore more significant in the institutional investment scene than they are to households, the ultimate wealth-holders. As will soon emerge, the effect of changes in the quantity of money on the two types of assets – variable-income and fixed-income – are different in scale and character, and the differences are important to the economy's cyclical behaviour.

How do the prices of housing and quoted equities, which epitomise variable-income assets, respond to changes in the quantity of money? Housing yields rents to homeowners, which may be either an actual rent paid by a tenant to a landlord, or an imputed rent when homes are occupied by their owners. A fair surmise is that – whatever form it takes – the dominant influence on the growth of rents is the increase in nominal national output. Moreover, the most neutral assumption in a model of economic growth would be that rents are stable relative to GDP. By contrast, two kinds of income streams are associated with corporate equity. These are profits, which may be retained within the business to finance investment or distributed to shareholders, and dividends, which are the amounts thus distributed. For each individual business, profits are variable, and depend on the energy, skill and efficiency of management. However, for the economy as a whole, success and failure even out. The long-run tendency in the US has been for the share of profits in GDP to be relatively stable, although perhaps with some tendency to rise in the last 20 or so years. (See Figure 1.)

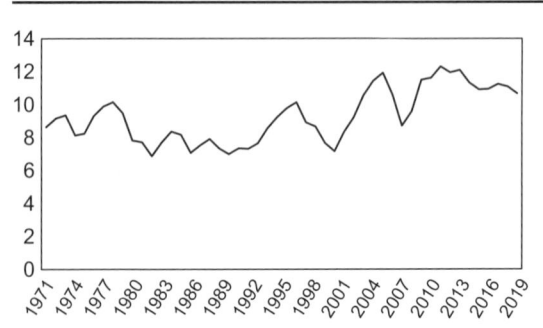

Figure 1 Corporate profits as a share of US GDP

[Chart showing values fluctuating between approximately 6 and 13 from 1971 to 2019]

Source: FRED database, provided by the Federal Reserve of St Louis website. Profits are after inventory valuation and consumption adjustments.

Proportionality postulate applies to variable-income assets

A reasonable assumption in theorising is that – given the data over many decades – the incomes paid on variable-income assets are a constant ratio of GDP. The realism of the assumption can be questioned, and it should not be pressed too far. All the same, it gives fewer hostages to fortune than a generalisation that incomes on variable-income assets change systematically relative to other incomes. The discussion in the last chapter noticed 'the proportionality postulate', that – in certain circumstances, once equilibrium has been established – changes in the quantity of money are associated with equi-proportional changes in nominal GDP. The necessary implication of the discussion is that, again in equilibrium, the value of all the variable-income assets in an economy rises or falls equi-proportionally with the quantity of money. This is hardly surprising. Asset values are the capitalisations of income streams. If money and national income change equi-proportionally, and if factor shares in national income are constant, the values of variable-income assets should conform to the proportionality postulate.

Table 3 Money, income and the value of variable-income assets in the US, 1946–2021

% annual compound increases over 75 years to 2021 in	
Personal disposable income	6.5
Money	7.0
Corporate equities	8.0
Non-corporate equity	5.7
Real estate	7.7
Real estate and business equity combined	7.3

See notes to Table 2, which has the same source.

Readers may feel that the step just taken is radical and far-reaching, and takes us into uncharted territory. But a side-glance at reality may justify more confidence in the idea being advanced. The US has data on household wealth extending back to the end of World War II. How do money, personal income and wealth relate over a long period in this emblematic capitalist nation? Table 3 shows that personal disposable income has increased in the 75 years to 2021 at a compound annual rate of 6.5%, rather less than that of corporate equity (most of it quoted) and real estate (mostly houses), which had compound annual rates of increase of 8.0% and 7.7% respectively. But non-corporate business equity – which would have had a big farming component in 1946 – went up at a lower compound annual rate of only 5.7%. If the three main types of variable-income asset are taken together, their compound annual rate of increase was 7.3%. The rate of increase in money, of 7.0% a year, lay between that of income and variable-income assets.

Let us take it that the evidence supports the suggestion that the proportionality postulate applies to variable-income assets, where such assets dominate household wealth. The suggestion becomes basic to the transmission mechanism in the real world. When the quantity of money goes up by, say, 10%, a reasonable conjecture is that the value of the stock market and the housing stock will also go up, probably over a few quarters, by a figure close to 10%. (In qualification, some 'over-shooting' in equity markets is common (Congdon 2021b). A discussion of the relationship between money growth and UK house prices in the Covid period is given in chapter 9.)

Moreover, at the end of 2021, business equity and residential housing were together worth more than five times personal disposable income in the year 2021 (see Table 2). When asset prices are strong, people can sell assets to pay for consumption above income and extensions to their homes, or to invest in any businesses they own; when they are weak, they may defer consumption and home improvements, stop expansion plans for small businesses, and save more out of income to boost accumulated wealth. *Pace* Samuelson, the transmission mechanism is not a black box at all. Through their impact on variable-asset prices, fluctuations in money growth are likely to have easily understood effects on demand, output and employment.

The relationships between changes in the quantity of money and changes in expenditure on 'commodities' or 'goods and services' – the relationships highlighted in the earlier excerpts from Wicksell and Friedman – might be termed the 'direct effects' from money in the transmission mechanism. The mechanism just elaborated might then be viewed as an 'indirect' one, since it works through asset markets before it hits expenditure in shops, over websites and so on. Notice that no rate of interest and no debt securities have been mentioned in the last four paragraphs. An indirect effect in the transmission mechanism has been identified and explained, without any references to 'the interest rate' or 'bond yields'. Tenreyro and Woodford may be unhappy about the omission, but arguably Woodford's 2003 book on *Interest and Prices* suffers from greater selectivity. That much-lauded volume relates to an economy without commercial banks, industrial and commercial companies, and non-bank financial institutions. (To be fair, Woodford has theorised about an economy with extensive financial intermediation (Woodford 2010), if with credit-based determination of national income.)

Textbooks' obsession with 'the rate of interest'

The points being made here may seem unsurprising – even fatuous – to readers active in business and finance who have never been taught any formal economics. But this area of economics, as it is learned in the classroom and from textbooks, is beset by an obsession with 'the rate of interest'. In the 1985 fourth edition of his widely admired *Economic Theory in Retrospect*, Mark Blaug blessed the remark that 'the quantity theory of money assigns no explicit role to the rate of interest and ... no monetary theory is worth very much if it neglects the interest rate' (Blaug 1985). He proceeded to the assertion that the indirect mechanism is about the effect of changes in money on the rate of interest and then the effect of changes in the rate of interest on expenditure, and by implication that it is only about these effects.

Blaug attributed the first presentation of the indirect mechanism to an 1802 book on *Paper Credit* by Henry Thornton, an English banker who flourished at the time of the Napoleonic Wars. But nowadays discussion in this area of economics tends to be dominated by Keynes's treatment in his *General Theory* or, at any rate, by expositions which remember and are heavily influenced by that treatment. In the introduction, when referring to Keynes's liquidity preference theory of 'the rate of interest' (that is, of a representative bond yield), it was explained that bond prices and yields move inversely. Via the bond yield and the fabled IS function, the stimulus to investment from an increase in the quantity of money became the key mechanism relating money to expenditure, output and employment. In the extreme, the Keynesians talk as if the IS function were the *only* link between money on the one side and national income and expenditure on the other. From here it is not far to Samuelson's puzzling denial that the quantity theory has a transmission mechanism, or to the assertions from Tenreyro and Woodford that the connection between monetary policy and inflation relies exclusively on interest rates and bond yields.[2]

But reality must intrude: this is an empirical matter. No one disputes that changes in bond yields affect the macroeconomic trajectory. The question is, how much? Let us take it – in line with several chapters in Keynes's *General Theory* – that at the centre of attention are the effects of a change in the quantity of money on the value of bonds and then of the change in the value of bonds on aggregate demand.[3] How might this be measured? One possible way is to obtain the relevant data for major cyclical episodes, and to quantify the relative importance of the Keynesian

---

2 Political – even ideological – commitments may be part of the trouble in this part of economics. In an encyclopaedia entry on the quantity theory, David Laidler (2002) suggested that the modern form of the quantity theory – or 'monetarism' – had political overtones, 'being linked to a "conservative" economic policy agenda in popular economic understanding'.

3 Keynes's *General Theory* had nothing to say about the determination of 'the interest rate', in the senses of either the central bank rate or the interbank rate. In this it was unlike the *Treatise on Money*, which has chapter 32 in the second volume devoted to it. To repeat, the interest rate in the *General Theory* was a bond yield. But, if the implicit premise of the *General Theory*'s treatment from chapter 13 onwards was that changes in the quantity of money affected only the prices of bonds and had no effect on the prices of other securities and assets, that was patently absurd in real-world financial markets. But Tenreyro and countless others seem to have been misled by the many Keynesian textbooks in which changes in the quantity of money affect only bond yields, and not the prices and yields of other assets. This has led to much theorising about the supposed ineffectiveness of monetary policy at low interest rates, with thousands of pages about such phantoms as 'the liquidity trap' and 'the lower bound'. The author's paper 'Can central banks run out of ammunition? The role of the money-into-equities interaction channel in monetary policy' (Congdon 2021b) denies the very possibility of the liquidity trap in an economy with a diverse range of non-money assets.

IS mechanism by comparing changes in the value of bonds with those in the value of variable-income assets. This is the purpose of Tables 4 and 5, which look at US household data for the period from end-2019 to end-2022, that is, roughly speaking, the period in which the Covid-19 medical emergency began and came under control.

Table 4   Capital gains and losses on variable-income assets in the US's Covid period

	Net holding gains (in billions of $s) from				
	Real estate	*Corporate equities*	*Mutual fund shares*	*Equity in non-corporate business*	*Selected variable-income assets in total*
2020:Q1	633	−4,798	−1,593	264	−5,493
2020:Q2	610	3,518	1,223	68	5,419
2020:Q3	722	1,768	532	294	3,316
2020:Q4	983	3,847	977	418	6,226
2021:Q1	1,243	1,800	332	483	3,857
2021:Q2	1,759	1,769	587	663	4,779
2021:Q3	1,887	188	−83	864	2,856
2021:Q4	770	1,278	446	596	3,089
2022:Q1	3,303	−1,018	−804	568	2,049
2022:Q2	2,135	−5,108	−1,493	673	−3,794
2022:Q3	−1,254	−1,016	−557	209	−2,618
2022:Q4	−978	1,182	534	−197	541

Personal disposable income was $16,388.6 billion in 2019 and $18,523.6 billion in 2022.

The value of variable-income assets in the US economy is taken to be the sum of the four columns in the left of the table. This is for illustration. There are further asset classes other than debt securities.

Source: US Federal Reserve *Financial Accounts of the United States* (June 2023 release), Table R101, p. 141.

Table 5 Capital gains and losses on major asset classes in the US's Covid period

	Net holding gains (in billions of $s) from		
	Selected variable-income assets in total	Debt securities	Change in value of variable-income assets as multiple of that in value of debt securities, without regard to sign.
2020:Q1	−5,493	121.3	45
2020:Q2	5,419	51.9	104
2020:Q3	3,316	−2.0	1,638
2020:Q4	6,226	5.2	1,205
2021:Q1	3,857	−121.9	32
2021:Q2	4,779	36.5	131
2021:Q3	2,856	−31.7	90
2021:Q4	3,089	−4.5	685
2022:Q1	2,049	−200.2	10
2022:Q2	−3,794	−122.0	31
2022:Q3	−2,618	−144.8	18
2022:Q4	541	53.6	10

Personal disposable income was $16,388.6 billion in 2019 and $18,523.6 billion in 2022.

Source: Same as Table 4.

Variable-income assets dominate bonds

Table 4 shows the four main kinds of variable-income asset owned by households and identified in the US data. It adds up the change in their value in the crucial period, which was of course one of great volatility as the alarm about Covid came and went. The final column has the total change in value of variable-income assets and is carried over to Table 5, which compares this number with the change in the value of debt securities. Table 5 computes changes in the value of variable-income assets held by households as a multiple of changes in the value of their debt securities. In some quarters the multiple is very high. *In the second half of 2020, changes in the value of households' variable-income assets were more than 1,000 times those in the value of their debt securities.* Crudely but inescapably, American households care far more about the stock market and house prices than they do about bond yields. Whatever some Keynesian economists – including Paul Samuelson – think about the matter, this is surely a commonplace with huge implications for macroeconomic analysis.[4] Households' decisions on their current and capital expenditure (that is, 'expenditure' in the income–expenditure flow, relevant to the national accounts), and on their investment portfolios, must be heavily influenced by their wealth and changes in its value. But such changes are – above all – changes in the value of variable-income assets.[5]

Declarations by prominent economists that monetary policy is only about interest rates and bond yields must be regarded as strange, to say the least. A fair comment on

---

4   In his first column for the American magazine *Newsweek*, in 1966, Samuelson joked that the stock market had predicted nine of the last five recessions.

5   The Samuelson textbook was clearly influenced by Keynes's *General Theory*. The author does not know if Samuelson read Keynes's other monetary writings, notably the 1923 *Tract on Monetary Reform* and the 1930 *Treatise on Money*, which had more quantity-theoretic material. (See Samuelson (1948: 303–4) for an early treatment from him of the effect of changes in the quantity of money on the rate of interest.) The author has argued that – via the textbook – Samuelson's economics, with its hostility to the quantity theory and monetary policy, has done much harm (Congdon 2022).

many Keynesian textbooks is that they ignore altogether the direct effect of changes in the quantity of money on the economy, while restricting the indirect effect in the transmission mechanism to that arising from the liquidity preference theory of bond yields. To the extent that they omit the direct effect(s) and restrict the indirect effect (or effects) to that working via bond yields plus the associated IS function, these textbooks are so misleading as to be wrong and dangerous.[6] (In the author's view, a forecast of the values of the equity market and the stock of residential houses, and indeed all important asset categories, has to be part of any meaningful macroeconomic forecast. The point is to be developed at more length in chapter 4 in his forthcoming book, *Money and Inflation at the Time of Covid*.)

The discussion has been intended to open eyes and broaden horizons. The majority of university students are taught from textbooks which purvey Keynesian macroeconomics and snub the quantity theory of money. Sometimes the economy consists only of the transactions in the so-called income–expenditure–output circular flow, which are said to determine GDP (Mankiw 2019: 16–18). The level of GDP implied by these transactions can then be viewed as stable and persistent, unless it is upset by unspecified and intermittent 'shocks' (Dow 1998: 38).

This is to caricature the real world. As Keynes himself was well aware, and as he spelt out fully in his *Treatise on Money*, the economy contains transactions in assets as

---

[6] See the section 'Dangers of three-equation New Keynesianism' beginning on p. 16 for more on the much-cited article by Clarida et al. (1999).

well as transactions in his 'industrial circulation'.[7] Transactions in assets, as well as a range of other transactions outside the circular flow, are so large that – to repeat – the value of transactions in a modern economy is a very high multiple of both those in the purported 'circular flow' and GDP itself.[8] Shocks from fluctuations in the value of securities and real estate are incessant, and imply that expenditure for some agents may sometimes have only a loose connection with their incomes. At the end of chapter 7 of his *General Theory*, Keynes reminded his readers that, while every individual has the freedom to change the amount of money in his or her possession, at the aggregate level it is logically necessary that

> the total amount of money, which individual balances add up to, ... be exactly equal to the amount of cash which the banking system has created.

Suppose that, for whatever reason, the quantity of money changes. Then,

> incomes and [the] prices of securities necessarily change until the aggregate of the amounts of money which individuals choose to hold at the new level of incomes and

---

7   The industrial circulation proposed in Keynes's *Treatise* might be understood as an anticipation of the income–expenditure so-called circular flow, which is a centrepiece of Keynesian textbook macroeconomics.

8   The image of a circle is hardly the right one for the flow of transactions in an economy. Asset prices are so volatile, as are incomes related to the value of asset transactions, that – for many agents – income and expenditure can behave quite differently for extended periods.

prices thus brought about has come to equality with the amount of money created by the banking system. This, indeed, is the fundamental proposition of monetary theory.

As Keynes saw, the price of 'securities' – in fact, assets of all kinds – had to be incorporated in his 'fundamental proposition of monetary theory' (Keynes 1973: 84–85). Unfortunately, later in the *General Theory* – specifically, in chapters 13–17, leading up to the synoptic chapter 18 on 'The general theory of employment restated' – Keynes lost his sense of the relative importance of different magnitudes. He embarked on a large-scale intellectual advertising campaign for his problematic liquidity preference theory of the rate of interest. The campaign was successful, in that it convinced the young Paul Samuelson. Via his textbook, Samuelson then bamboozled three generations of economists into believing that bond yields held the key to understanding macroeconomic instability.

Lags between money and inflation

One more issue needs to be discussed before closing this account of the monetary transmission mechanism. The argument has been that – after a period of time, in which the economy is in disequilibrium – a shock to the quantity of money results in equi-proportional changes in national income and expenditure, and in the value of variable-income assets, as equilibrium is restored. But how long is that period of time?

As usual in this subject, Friedman had views and expressed them lucidly. To quote (Blaug et al. 1995: 42):

> For most Western economies a change in the rate of monetary growth produces a change in the rate of growth of nominal income about six to nine months later ... The effect on prices, like that on income and output, comes some twelve to eighteen months later, so that the total delay between a change in monetary growth and a change in the rate of inflation averages something like two years ... In the short run, which may be as long as three to ten years, monetary changes primarily affect output. Over decades, on the other hand, the rate of monetary growth affects primarily prices.

Friedman was certainly exercised by the lags in money transmission and wrote much about them. While the passage quoted is representative, it was not the only view he held. Indeed, Edward Nelson, writing as a Federal Reserve economist, noted in an intellectual biography of Friedman that his handling of the subject was sometimes 'precarious' and 'with evidence of backtracking' (Nelson 2020: 232–37). All the same (ibid.: 238):

> The two-year rule of thumb for the reaction of inflation to monetary policy actions, which entered Friedman's framework at the end of 1971 and became a staple part of it thereafter, has ... since become a standard part of practical monetary analysis.

THE TRANSMISSION MECHANISM

The two-year rule of thumb has the merit of definiteness. However, an argument can be made that it is too definite. In practice, the effect of a change in money growth on the economy will depend critically on how much unemployment and spare capacity it has or, in a phrase, on the so-called output gap.[9] An acceleration of *x plus* 2% in the rate of money growth may have little or no adverse impact on inflation for several quarters, if output is initially much beneath trend. Conversely, an acceleration of *x minus* 2% in the rate of money growth may be followed by an early and abrupt acceleration of *x minus* 2% in the rate of inflation if output is well above trend. The Friedman generalisation might be viewed as a statement of the likely outcome if the economy is starting from approximate monetary equilibrium, with output at trend. Taken this way, it turns out to be useful in understanding the Covid-related cyclical upheaval of the early 2020s. However, the lags between an upturn in money growth and inflation in the UK's two big boom–bust cycles of the late twentieth century were double Friedman's figure of two years (see Congdon 2007: 243, footnote 9).[10]

---

[9] The notion of 'the output gap' is ambiguous. Two very different versions are in common use, one arising from Keynesian thought and the other from a monetarist approach. See essay 6 in Congdon (2011). The reference in the text is to the monetarist concept of the gap, as this is the notion used by the IMF.

[10] The money/inflation lag in the Heath–Barber boom of the early 1970s and the Lawson boom of the late 1980s was about four years.

7 SOME EVIDENCE FOR THE QUANTITY THEORY OF MONEY

The discussion of lags completed our account of the money transmission mechanism in the last two chapters. Already it had become necessary to look at patterns in the real world, such as the length of the lags in the transmission mechanism. The purpose of this chapter is to select and present more data on the money–GDP relationship, although – of course – these data are only a tiny fraction of what is available. Three bodies of evidence are examined: the US household wealth numbers already discussed; the relationship between money growth and inflation for the G20 countries from 1980 to 2022; and the relationship decade by decade of the growth rates of money and nominal GDP in the US. Basic to the whole subject is the validity of the proportionality postulate. Roughly speaking, the postulate is valid if and where – over the medium and long runs, when the economy has had time to equilibrate the demand to hold money with the quantity of money actually in being – the rates of change of money, broadly defined, and of national income and wealth are similar. It will turn out that a major qualification has to be mentioned, but this qualification does not disturb the intellectual integrity of the quantity theory of money.

Table 6 Changes in US household sector balance sheet, 1946–2021

	Value at end-2021, as multiple of value at end-1946
Money, mostly deposits	155.9
Total financial assets	167.7
Total assets, before debt	182.3
Total liabilities	490.2
Total assets after debt	169.3
Personal disposable income	111.9
....	
Ratio of money to annual income	1.39
Ratio of net assets to annual income	1.51
Ratio of gross assets to annual income	1.63
Ratio of all liabilities to annual income	4.38

Source: Data downloaded from Federal Reserve flow-of-funds database, at September 2023, and author's calculations. Annual income is that in final quarters of 1946 and 2021 multiplied by four.

US households in the long run

Recall Table 3, which demonstrated the long-run similarity of the rates of increase in the US household sector's income, money holdings and holdings of variable-income assets. There is more to say. Table 6 shows that, in the 75 years from 1946 to 2021, American households increased their money holdings almost 146 times, while their incomes rose about 112 times. So the ratio between the two was not constant, but its change – of just under 40% – was modest relative to the multiplications of both money and incomes. Further, an explanation was available for the rise in the money/income ratio. In this 75-year period American households became richer not just in absolute terms, but also with wealth growing relative to income. The net wealth-to-income ratio moved up from 5.4 in 1946 to 8.1 in 2021. On top of that, financial behaviour became more complicated. At the end of World War II, households had little debt, but by 2021 liabilities of all sorts were roughly the same size as annual income.[1] Plainly, financial transactions – transactions mostly in existing assets – must have increased relative to transactions in the income–expenditure flow. It becomes logical that, as a by-product of 'financialisation', money holdings should have increased in a typical year a bit faster than incomes.

As the US has a fairly representative capitalist economy, the behaviour of its households over three generations provides a worthwhile insight into people's attitudes more generally towards their money holdings.

A more international perspective

Readers may nevertheless want information that relates to a larger and more diverse group of economies. At the time of writing (March 2024), the home page of the Institute of International Monetary Research carries a chart of the relationship between money and inflation for the G20 from 1980 to 2022. Specifically, it gives the annual compound growth rates of broad money and nominal

---

[1] The peak ratio of liabilities to income was in 2007, at almost 1.4, just ahead of the Great Financial Crisis. But the net-wealth-to-income ratio in 2007 was higher than it had been at any time before the 1980s.

GDP in this period of just over 40 years for these nations. Figure 2 reproduces this chart and gives key features of the ordinary-least-squares regression equation of the relationship shown. The message is unmistakeable: nations which had rapid growth of money also had rapid growth of nominal GDP, and often this meant much inflation, whereas nations with low growth of money had similarly low growth of nominal GDP.

The policy implications of Figure 2 are also unmistakeable. If nations have an inflation problem, the problem is not an innate national characteristic. Everywhere in the world a programme of monetary restraint which reduces money growth close to that of national output will prevent inflation. References to certain structural non-monetary aspects of various economies may throw light on the difficulties of introducing programmes of this kind. But these structural non-monetary aspects are not the cause of the inflation from which places like Argentina and Turkey have suffered for so long.

The US over the medium term

A common claim from critics of the quantity theory is that the demand to hold money has become unstable in recent decades. This claim often relies on elaborate econometric tests and appears in complex academic articles that bewilder non-academics. As a corrective to such obfuscation, it may help to show – decade by decade – the growth rates of money and nominal GDP in one major country. Here the US is chosen, with Table 7 starting in 1960.

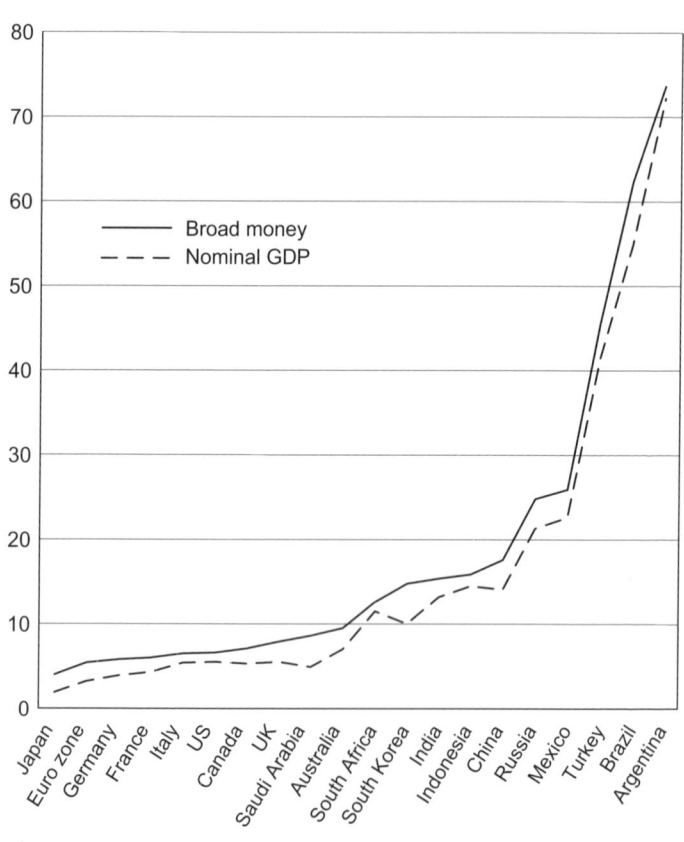

Figure 2 Money growth and inflation in the G20, 1980–2022

Ordinary-least-squares equation of the relationship shown in the chart, between the compound annual % growth rates of broad money and nominal GDP in the G20 countries, 1980–2022.

% annual change in nominal GDP = −1.96 + 0.96% annual change in broad money; r^2 = 0.995; t statistic on regression coefficient = 57.8; t statistic on intercept term = −4.4.

Source: Data from IMF and author's calculations.

Table 7 Decadal growth rates of money and nominal GDP in the US from 1960

	% annual growth rate	
	M3 broad money	Nominal GDP
1960–2023	7.4	6.4
1960–1970	7.7	6.8
1971–1980	11.4	10.3
1981–1990	7.7	7.7
1991–2000	5.6	5.6
2001–2010	7.1	3.9
2011–2020	5.6	3.6
2011–2019	4.0	4.0
2011–2023	5.5	4.8

Sources: FRED database at St Louis Fed for nominal GDP and M3 until 2006. M3 thereafter from Shadow Government Statistics. The quarterly M3 numbers are those for the middle month of the quarter.

As the table shows, over the entire period of almost 65 years, the growth rate of money was about 1% a year faster than that of nominal GDP, but – given our discussion of the financialisation of American households – that should not come as a surprise. A conspicuous feature of Table 7 is that the three decades (that is, those from 1960 to 1990) with the highest average money growth rate of 8.9% also had the highest average growth rate of nominal GDP of 8.3%. The 1970s are egregious, with the highest growth rates of money and nominal GDP, and in fact inflation. After 1990 money growth was typically lower, and so were inflation and the increases in nominal GDP.

The decade 2011–20 was distorted by its final year, 2020, the year of course of the Covid pandemic. In the year to mid 2020, M3 soared by 25.1%, whereas nominal GDP dropped by 6.9%. Although this was only one quarter out of 40 it was enough to affect the decadal averages. Table 7 therefore gives numbers also for the 9 years 2011–19 inclusive, when the growth rates of broad money and nominal GDP were identical, and for the 13 years 2011–23 inclusive. The anomaly of 2020 still affected the longer 13-year period, but the growth rates of broad money and nominal GDP were much closer at 5.5% and 4.8% respectively.

Summarising the evidence

The evidence surveyed is overwhelmingly in favour of the quantity theory. However, in one respect the proportionality postulate did not work. As noticed, in the US, households' money increased slightly faster than households' income, with the argument being that money was needed for financial transactions that tend to grow more rapidly than incomes. The same sort of pattern might also be identified in the G20 evidence. The value of the coefficient on money in the OLS equation reported in Figure 2 is not 1, but 0.96, while the intercept term of minus 1.96 achieves the usual test for statistical significance.[2] The G20 result is therefore that money tends to rise faster than national income over the medium and long terms.

---

[2] For those unfamiliar with econometric practice, a t statistic on the coefficient of 2 is usually taken to be necessary for significance. The coefficient on the intercept term is over 4.

A repeated pattern is that the 'banking habit' spreads in the take-off stage of economic development, and complements the rises in productivity and living standards. Even after most companies and people have bank accounts, the process of financialisation – already mentioned in the US context – is commonly found in all market economies. In summary, when broad money is used as the favoured money aggregate, the strict proportionality postulate does not hold in many surveys of real-world experience. Instead a standard feature of the data is that the income velocity of money falls in the medium and long runs, as an associate of the increase in financial interdependence which accompanies economic growth.

Readers may be impressed by the evidence just presented. As a result, they may be flummoxed by some economists' dismissiveness towards both money as an element in the macroeconomic debate and the quantity theory of money more particularly (see, for example, Bernanke 2022: 35–36, 141–43). They are right to be flummoxed, but they should perhaps be warned that the evidence has been chosen in order to bolster the persuasiveness of this restatement of the quantity theory.[3] Other evidence is less compelling. Disputes about the strength of the relationship between money and inflation have been almost

---

3 The household sector has a more stable demand to hold money balances than companies or financial institutions. So the choice of the US household sector to demonstrate stable underlying behaviour is to bias the analysis. It is well-known that the relationship between money and nominal GDP is better in low-frequency work than in high-frequency work. So a regression of compound growth rates *over 40 or so years* (that is, at a very low frequency) again helps to deliver a result favourable to the quantity theory.

continuous since the first glimmerings of quantity-theory conceptualising in the sixteenth century.[4]

Nevertheless, the naysayers can go too far. Princeton's Paul Krugman, with his column in the *New York Times*, is widely regarded as the world's most influential economist. In May 2021 he used his column to sneer at the handful of pundits who had worried about the inflationary dangers implicit in excessive money growth.[5] Krugman drew a distinction between 'zombie ideas', which shamble along 'eating people's brains', and the much worse 'cockroach ideas', which despite their falsity 'always come back'. Monetarists' claim of a connection between money and inflation was – according to Krugman – merely a cockroach idea. In his words, the then-emerging 'buzz' about the subject was evidence of 'an infestation of monetary cockroaches'. Might one ask whether Krugman – a Nobel laureate – indulged in this sort of thing for instruction or entertainment?

---

[4] For a trenchant recent verdict in favour of the quantity theory, see Hanke (2023).

[5] Paul Krugman, 'Krugman wonks out: return of the monetary cockroaches', *New York Times*, 13 May 2021.

8 APPLYING THE THEORY TO THE US IN THE EARLY 2020s

We have restated the quantity theory of money and presented evidence for the restated version. How, then, could it be applied in spring and summer 2020 to make strong forecasts of rising inflation in the medium term? More detailed narratives are available in the work which the author did shortly after the Covid emergency was announced, but they would take up space.[1] An appendix to this chapter gives most of a special e-mail sent out on 30 March 2020 to subscribers to the Institute of International Monetary Research. Nevertheless, it is appropriate now to develop the key points in those narratives, with the focus in this chapter on the US situation and in the next on the UK.[2]

---

1 The author's planned book *Money and Inflation at the Time of Covid*, to be published in 2025, will have more on these topics.

2 For the UK, see the next chapter. The author has written less about the euro zone, but see Congdon (2021c). The answer to the question in that paper – 'Does the upturn in Eurozone money growth imply 5% inflation?' – was 'yes', when most forecasts were for inflation to remain indefinitely in the low single digits. In fact, the peak in consumer price inflation in October 2022 was 10.6%.

Covid shatters monetary equilibrium

After the turbulence of the Great Recession, the US economy had much more stable policies in the years leading up to mid 2019. In the seven and a half years to June 2019 the average annual growth rate of M3 broad money was 4.1%, with a standard deviation over that period of 0.9.[3] As measured by the standard deviation, money-growth volatility was much less than had been common in most of the preceding century. Indeed, Table 8 shows that the volatility of growth of both money and nominal GDP was lower in these seven-and-a-half years in the 2010s than in any of the previous seven-and-a-half-year periods since World War I. On the face of it, the table provides evidence to support the case for a constant-money-growth rule of the kind favoured by Friedman and others, but further discussion of this very important topic is beyond the scope of the present study.

According to the International Monetary Fund, the US's national output was at trend in 2018, while in 2019 it was only marginally (0.7% of trend output) above trend (IMF 2023). A reasonable view is that in mid 2019 the American economy was in or close to 'monetary equilibrium', as that phrase was used in chapter 4. An upturn in money growth

---

3   The standard deviation was calculated from a series of annual growth rates on a quarterly basis. A regression of the data in Table 7 – that is, of the standard deviations of nominal GDP growth on the standard deviations of money growth in the 13 periods of 7½ years to mid 2019 – was surprisingly good. The positive regression coefficient of 1.37 had a t statistic of 8.49, while the coefficient of determination (r^2) was 0.93. But the analysis, while suggestive, needs amplification to establish the case for the constant-money-growth rule.

occurred in the nine months from spring 2019, but this was minor compared with what was to follow. At the end of February 2020 the M3 measure of broad money was just under $21,000 billion, a figure which is a key marker for the next few paragraphs.

Table 8 The stability of the growth rates of money and nominal GDP in the US in the twentieth and twenty-first centuries

	Standard deviations in the 7½ year periods of	
	Broad money	*Nominal GDP*
1922–mid 1929	3.7	6.7
Mid 1929–end 1936	11.6	16.1
1937–mid 1944	8.5	11.8
Mid 1944–1951	6.9	8.3
1952–mid 1959	1.5	3.6
Mid 1959–end 1966	4.3	2.1
1967–mid 1974	1.5	2.1
Mid 1974–end 1981	2.0	2.0
1982–mid 1989	2.3	2.3
Mid 1989–end 1996	2.3	1.2
1997–mid 2004	2.2	1.5
Mid 2004–end 2011	5.0	2.9
2012–mid 2019	0.9	0.9

The data used are of annual growth rates %, on a quarterly basis.

A salient feature of the data is that the extreme instability of money growth in the early 1930s coincided with the Great Depression. Stable money growth in the 1950s, the Great Moderation and the final period ('the Great Stabilisation') was accompanied by relatively stable growth of nominal GDP.

Source: Contact the author at timcongdon@btinternet.com for the sources, which are numerous and rather various.

The Covid-19 medical emergency was announced by President Trump on 13 March, amid sliding prices and panic on the stock market, and widespread pessimism and alarm about the economic future. The federal deficit started to widen dramatically, partly because of the loss of tax revenue, but also because of extra expenditure to mitigate the effects of the virus. The American central bank, the Federal Reserve, made clear its preparedness to finance the much-enlarged budget deficit and also undertook large-scale asset purchases (or 'quantitative easing') to stabilise financial markets.

Money explosion

Stimulatory announcements – of both fiscal and monetary policy, and including QE – came through thick and fast in the closing weeks of March and all through April. It was soon clear that the CARES (Coronavirus Aid, Relief and Economic Security) legislation would have a cost of roughly $2,300 billion in the 2020 and 2021 fiscal years combined (Penn Wharton Budget Model 2020). With other measures, the federal deficit was likely to exceed $3,000 billion for an extended period and might even reach $4,000 billion. In the event, the cumulative 12 month total for the federal deficit peaked at $4,320 billion in April 2021, and exceeded $2,900 billion from June 2020 to October 2021. If two-thirds of a deficit of $3,000 billion were financed from the banks, that meant an addition to broad money of $2,000 billion *in one year*, just under 10% of the M3 stock at end-February.

But on top of that, the Fed committed itself to enormous QE operations. The asset purchases were on a particularly large scale in late March and April, and were openly advertised as having the purpose of checking the slide in financial markets, including the stock market. The Federal Reserve financed the asset purchases by issuing cash reserves to the commercial banks, which became part of their assets. In the eight weeks from 26 February 2020 and 22 April 2020 the cash reserves held by US commercial banks at the Fed soared from $1,705.2 billion to $3,234.1 billion. The extra assets had to be matched, mostly, by extra deposit liabilities, and deposits are money. So the Fed's operations implied an addition to broad money – within about two months – of over 7%. Further, in the early weeks of the crisis companies drew down credit lines, from fear that a worsening crisis might impair banks' solvency and hence their ability to extend credit. 'Loans and leases in bank credit' – a category in Federal Reserve data which corresponds to bank lending to the private sector – climbed from $10,070 billion on 26 February to $10,874.6 billion ten weeks later. This change too added about 4% to banks' assets and their deposit liabilities.

An explosion in money growth was implied by the Fed's and US government's announcements in late March, and their actions as the announcements took effect. Admittedly, the exact sequence and scale of official operations were uncertain, but – as the last two paragraphs have shown – it was not silly to propose that altogether the positive impact on broad money might be well above 30% in two years.

Table 9 The arithmetic of the US's 2020 money explosion

At the end of February 2020, the US M3 measure of money was just under $21,000 billion.

1. The fiscal cost of the CARES legislation

In the 2019 fiscal year (the year to September 2019) the Federal deficit was $865.3 billion, while in the year to February 2020 it reached $1,298.6 billion. The expected cost of the CARES legislation, passed on 27 March 2020, was given as $2,200 billion, mostly to affect the 2020 and 2021 fiscal years.

By implication, the Federal deficit would move out to $3,000 billion or more for at least two years.

The Federal Reserve indicated its preparedness to finance the deficit. If two-thirds of the deficit (at an annual rate of $3,000 billion) were financed from the banking sytem, **broad money would increase by almost 10%.**

2. Federal Reserve asset purchases

The Federal Reserve made announcements of large-scale asset purchases to stabilise financial markets.

On 15 March the Fed said it would buy at least $500 billion of Treasuries and $200 billion in mortgage-backed securities (MBSs) in coming months. On 23 March the purchases became open-ended and, potentially, unlimited. The New York Fed even spoke in terms of $100 billion a day, i.e. perhaps over $500 billion in one week. In June the rate of purchases was reduced to $80 billion of Treasuries and $40 billion of MBSs per month.

If $200 billion of asset purchases are from non-banks, the increase in M3 would be 1%.

The addition to M3 from the asset purchases depends on the proportion of purchases from non-banks. But an extra 3–4% on M3 at an annual rate was plausible in the circumstances of spring 2020.

3. Drawing-down of credit lines in the early weeks of the crisis

See text. 'Loans and leases in bank credit' rose by just over $800 billion in the 10 weeks from 26 February.

This increased broad money by almost 4%.

Calculation of the combined effect of the three developments

Effect estimated in one-year period	$ billions	% effect on M3
Prospective fiscal cost, with monetisation	2000	+9 to +10
Fed asset purchases	600–800	+3 to +4
Credit drawdown	800	+4
Indicated effect in total	**3,400–3,600**	**+16 to +18**

Drawdown of credit lines was a one-off, non-recurring item affecting only 2020. In thinking about the % change M3 broad money in 2021, an allowance would have to be made for the much higher base level of M3 at the end of 2020.

The consequent rate of money growth – of perhaps over 15% a year – would be much higher than the 4% recorded for most of the 2010s.[4] In the event M3 went up by more in *the one month* of April 2020 than it had in *any full year* in the 2010s. Given the analysis in the preceding sections of this chapter, and given also the monetary theory of national income determination developed in chapters 2–6, a forecast could be given that the policy response to the Covid-19 medical emergency would result in an inflationary boom. Figure 3, which gives the three-month annualised rate of increase of M3 from the Great Recession to June 2020, indicates the speed and abruptness of the break in money growth in spring 2020.

---

[4] In the event M3 growth in the two years from February 2020 was 32.4%, but – surprisingly – much of it was compressed into the mere five months from February to July 2020. (The author wishes – once more – to thank the Shadow Government Statistics consultancy for the M3 numbers.)

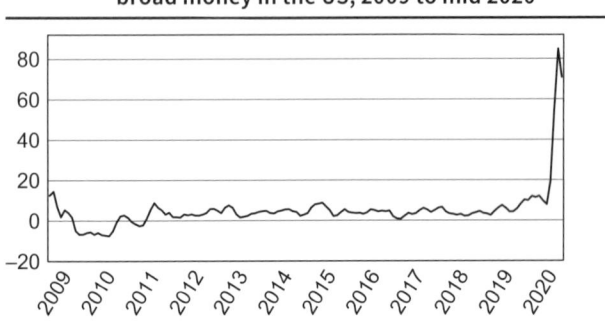

Figure 3 Three-month annualised growth rate % of M3 broad money in the US, 2009 to mid 2020

Risks of double-digit inflation

With the American economy starting from approximate monetary equilibrium in late 2019 and early 2020, that money explosion would result – if Friedman's proposed two-year lag turned out right – in a probable inflation peak in summer and autumn 2022. As the annual rate of money growth would almost certainly be in the teens per cent, a high risk of double-digit inflation had arisen. The outcome was not far from this conjecture. The annual rate of increase in the consumer price index – which had averaged just above 1.5% in the 12 years to end-2020 – was 7.2% at the end of 2021 and peaked at 8.9% in June 2022. It has fallen since then, but at the time of writing (March 2024) remains above the approximate 2% target that the Fed once set itself. (The annual increase in the so-called 'final demand producer price index' – a measure of prices at factory gates – reached a local peak of 11.7% in April

2022. The average annual increase in the five years to December 2019 – before Covid and the money explosion – was 1.3%.)

Did the Federal Reserve understand what it was doing? Were any internal warnings given – using an analytical approach to monetary policy of the sort proposed in this book – that the additions to broad money due to the Fed's decisions were likely to culminate in an inflation rate close to double digits? On Thursday, 26 March 2020, Jay Powell, the Fed's chair, was interviewed by Savannah Guthrie of the *Today* television programme. He was asked, 'Is there any limit to the amount of money that the Fed is willing to put it into the economy to keep it afloat?' Powell's response included the following words: 'Essentially, the answer to your question is no' (Smialek 2023: 190).

Fed chairman denies that 'money matters'

By early 2021 Federal Reserve economists must have heard at least whispers of outside concern about the inflationary potential of recent rapid money growth in the US. But they seem to have instructed Powell about how to dismiss any such concern. In February Powell (then aged 68) was given the opportunity – in his Semiannual Monetary Policy Report to Congress – to express his views on money and inflation. In reply to a question from Senator John Kennedy (aged 69), he was vigorous in rejecting basic principles of supposedly old-fashioned monetary economics (Senate Committee on Banking, Housing and Urban Affairs 2021). To quote:

> When you and I studied economics a million years ago M2 and monetary aggregates seemed to have a relationship to economic growth. Right now ... M2 ... does not really have important implications. It is something we have to unlearn I guess.

In further Congressional testimony in December 2021, he had the chance to recant, but instead doubled down on his previous position. The link between money and inflation had, in Powell's words, 'ended about 40 years ago'. In more detail:

> Now, we think more of just the imbalances between supply and demand in the real economy rather than monetary aggregates. ... It's been a different economy and a different financial system for some time.[5]

Almost certainly the source of Powell's ideas was advice from the New Keynesian economists at the Fed. Their research focus was not on the money aggregates, but rather the role of labour market imperfections in wage-setting.

---

5 The remarks appeared in evidence to the House of Representatives' Committee of Financial Services on 1 December 2021.

9 APPLYING THE THEORY TO THE UK IN THE EARLY 2020s

From an economic perspective, the years in the UK from 1992 to 2007 have been widely termed 'the Great Moderation'. Low inflation matched the official target set out in legislation, while coinciding with steady, quite high output growth. The years from 2007 to mid 2012 were much more troubled and might be seen as 'the Great Recession' and its aftermath. On the same basis, the period from mid 2012 to the start of 2020 could be described as 'the Great Stabilisation'. As in the Great Moderation, UK annual consumer price inflation stayed within the band of 1–3% specified in the legislation, except for 21 months between December 2014 and September 2016. In these 21 months inflation was between 0 and 1%, with the undershoot attracting little criticism or concern.

The Great Stabilisation of the 2010s

The undershoot could be attributed – in a cost-breakdown analysis – partly to extreme weakness in commodity prices and, in particular, to energy prices. To some extent, these developments reflected global forces outside the control of

UK policymakers. But also relevant and more fundamental was sluggish money growth. In the six years to the end of 2014 (that is, to just before the 21 months of sub-1% inflation), the average annual growth rate of the M4x broad money was 2.9%. The 2.9% figure was the lowest over such an extended interval of time since the inter-war period.

The Great Stabilisation is surely a fair characterisation, but the period should not be confused with heaven on earth. Supply-side performance – the average growth rate of output of the British economy over the years – was mediocre. But the stability of the growth from year to year was impressive and certainly matched the achievement of the Great Moderation. Further, after the undershoot in the middle of the decade, inflation remained on target. Arguably, the very satisfactory UK inflation outcome in the 2010s was consistent with the standard monetarist conjecture. Specifically, the velocity of circulation was not constant, but changes in it were much less than those in either the quantity of money or nominal GDP.

Indeed, a remarkable and very important feature of these years has been overlooked in public discussion, but is crucial to the main claims of the present study. In the 1970s Britain's monetarists – like their Chicago-based counterparts – advocated low and stable growth of the quantity of money, to be secured by officially announced targets. From 1979 the Thatcher government responded to these ideas, and pursued an avowedly monetarist programme to combat inflation. Low and stable growth of the quantity of money was seen as the heart of monetary management in the UK. In practice, targets and outturns were often far apart. All the same, the official focus on money growth deceleration did lead to a drop in inflation to about 5% a year. But from 1985 the targets were abandoned, and both money growth and inflation accelerated back towards double digits.[1] (The average annual increase in consumer prices in the Labour government from March 1974 to May 1979, which preceded Thatcher, was 15.8%.)

Curiously, it was in the Great Stabilisation of the 2010s – many years later – that the British government and the Bank of England took decisions that did in fact procure low and stable growth of the quantity of money, on the broad definitions. They did this, even though they thought they were doing something quite different. Anyhow, as monetarist economists had hoped and expected, steady, non-inflationary growth of demand and output was secured.

The Covid shock

As Covid-19 hit in early 2020, the Bank of England's top officials were in constant communication with other central bankers, both in Europe and the US. In the early weeks and months of the pandemic, policy announcements from the major central banks were similar. On 19 March the Bank's Monetary Policy Committee endorsed £200 billion of asset purchases, to be split between government securities and corporate bonds. On 18 June it added a further £100 billion to the total. A small proportion of the purchases were of

---

[1] The story of the rise and fall of money-target-focused monetarism in the UK is told in the author's 1992 collection, *Reflections on Monetarism* (Congdon 1992).

corporate bonds, but government securities were much more important. The stock of gilts held by the Bank of England's asset purchase facility was stable in the three years to the start of 2020 at just above £371 billion. The figure soared in the eight months to October 2020 by just under £214 billion to £585 billion.

A discussion in a footnote to chapter 3 explained the background and rationale to the estimation of the UK's M4x measure of broad money, and defended its usefulness for analytical purposes. M4x was slightly above £2,250 billion at February 2020. Official asset purchases of £200 billion might be as much as 75% from UK non-banks, implying an increase to M4x of £150 billion. So this £150 billion translated into a rise in M4x of just under 7%. If that rise were compressed into a mere three-month period, the annualised rate of money growth would be over 30% or so. In the event M4x rose by 7.3% in the three months to May, giving an annualised rate of growth of 32.8%. The annual increase – which had been a moderate 4.5% in February – was 12.5% in July. These numbers were plainly disruptive relative to the experience of the 2010s, but received few mentions in the media and no comment at all in the Bank's own publications.

From its inception in late 1992, the UK's inflation-target regime included the publication of a quarterly *Inflation Report* by the Bank of England, the first of which appeared in February 1993. But in November 2019, the results of the Monetary Policy Committee's deliberations were produced instead in a *Monetary Policy Report*, with the renaming of the report at least hinting that inflation was seen as yesterday's problem. The August 2020 *Monetary Policy Report* contained no reference to the acceleration in money growth, but did note that recent consumer inflation was

> well below the 2% target and was expected to fall further below it in coming quarters, largely reflecting the weakness of demand. At [its latest] meeting, the MPC judged that a further easing of monetary policy was warranted to meet its statutory objectives.

The judgement at the November MPC meeting remained that – in the next two years – inflation was more likely to undershoot than overshoot the 2% target. The MPC hence decided on another round of asset purchases, this time of £150 billion. Over the next year the Bank's asset purchase facility did climb, almost exactly, by another £150 billion. In the following months the annual rate of M4x money growth went up further, reaching a peak of 15.3% in February 2021. This was the highest number, on the annual growth metric, since M4x had been introduced as an aggregate in 1998. In fact, broad money growth had not been as strong – in the mid teens per cent at an annual rate – since the Lawson boom of the late 1980s, more than 30 years earlier.

Official worries in early 2021 about *de*flation!

As in the US and other advanced countries, most high-level research and macroeconomic conversations in the UK were – through 2020 and even early 2021 – about the risks that Covid would result in persistent deflation. Many respected observers applauded a big increase in the budget deficit as well as the Bank of England's asset purchases. Writing in the *Financial Times* on 22 June, Gavyn Davies, former chief London economist at Goldman Sachs, opined that the resulting rise in public debt should be viewed as a 'shock absorber'. His judgement was that governments' response to the crisis, in the UK as elsewhere, enjoyed 'a chorus of approval from the [economics] profession'.[2] To quote again from its August 2020 *Monetary Policy Report*, the Bank of England said that it envisaged inflation rising in coming quarters, as the economy recovered from Covid and 'spare capacity diminishes'. The rise in inflation would be from annual rates of under 1% at the time of the report's preparation and a further dip to about zero in early 2021. Consumer inflation was expected 'to be around 2 per cent in two years' time [that is, in August 2022]'.

Members of the Monetary Policy Committee gave speeches in late 2020 in which the worry was the possible inability of monetary policy to stimulate the economy and to take it out of the Covid slump.[3] For example, Michael Saunders participated in an online webinar on 4 December in which he set out, to cite the title of his speech, 'Some

---

[2] Gavyn Davies, Finding a strategy for public debt in the crisis, *Financial Times*, 22 June 2020.

[3] The intellectual background here is still dominated by the notion of 'absolute liquidity preference', and hence 'the liquidity trap', which go back to Keynes. See footnote 15 on p. 14 of the introduction and footnote 3 on p. 81 of the main text for more on this topic.

monetary policy options – if more support was needed'. Even though Bank rate could not fall much further, the MPC stood ready 'to take whatever additional action' might be needed 'if the outlook for inflation weakens'. M4x had risen by 13.6% in the year to November, but there was no hint that a serious future problem would be above-target inflation. Although Saunders's speech was said not necessarily to represent the MPC majority, it reflected the kind of thinking that had led to the announcement of the extra £150 billion of asset purchases.[4]

In summary, the overwhelming consensus among British economists in 2020 – and even as late as spring 2021 – was that Covid-19 would be followed by a long period of disinflation. The widespread expectation was a period of a few years in which policymakers' main preoccupation would be combating beneath-target inflation. Few economists paid much attention to money data, but an exception was the Shadow Monetary Policy Committee under the aegis of the London-based think tank, the Institute of Economic Affairs. The Committee's members became concerned about excessive money growth and sent a letter to the *Financial Times* noticing the similarity of the latest money growth patterns to those in the last big period of cyclical excess over 30 years earlier. The letter appeared

---

[4] By contrast, the author's monthly YouTube video for the Institute of International Monetary Research in November 2020 (https://www.youtube.com/watch?v=LUNTa1FRU5k&list=PLudZPVEs3S82lh5QYlWNegc0hEOzg2hH7&index=17) included an explicit warning that the 'money growth rate is too high – and is likely to lead, for a few quarters, to an annual inflation rate above 5%'.

in the *Financial Times* on 26 April 2021 under the heading 'BoE [Bank of England] must end its asset purchases to avoid stoking inflation'. To quote:

> We believe that above-target inflation is to be expected in 2022 and perhaps 2023. In our view, the Bank of England will be to blame for this setback, as it took the measures that have pushed money growth to its current excessive level ... We fear that inflation above 5 per cent is likely at some point in the next few years. We judge that the MPC's decision in November 2020 to embark on another round of quantitative easing, to the tune of £150bn, has proved particularly responsible for the current excessive money growth.

But the real Monetary Policy Committee had little or no interest in the behaviour of the quantity of money. A few weeks before the SMPC letter, Gertjan Vlieghe, an external member of the MPC, had given an update on the economic outlook at Durham University. His assessment was still that the 'pandemic shock was fundamentally a disinflationary shock'. Without the official stimulus measures, a 'severe disinflation' would have eventuated. In his view, the stimulus had been applied and 'inflation is expected to return sustainably to target' (Vlieghe 2021). He referred not once to any concept of the quantity of money and evidently did not believe that the attainment of target inflation required an appropriately low rate of money growth. Almost exactly a month after the SMPC letter, Silvana Tenreyro, an economist who had joined the MPC in 2017 and has already been mentioned in chapters 5 and 6, gave the keynote speech at a San Francisco conference. She compared policymakers' response to Covid in the US and the UK, and noted the commonality of diagnosis and prescription. She referred to UK households' 'liquid asset balances' and wondered about how quickly they would be spent, but not to their money holdings and the equilibrium ratio of such holdings to income and wealth (Tenreyro 2021).

Haldane's dissent

In fairness to the Bank of England, it has to be noticed that some in-house dissent from the majority view had emerged by early 2021. Andy Haldane, the Bank's chief economist, had started to have reservations about the MPC's consensus on never-ending low inflation. These were expressed in a noteworthy speech on 26 February (Haldane 2021). To quote from its final paragraphs:

> Inflation is the tiger whose tail central banks control. This tiger has been stirred by the extraordinary events and policy actions of the past 12 months ... [If] risks from the virus or elsewhere prove more persistent than expected, disinflationary forces could return. But, for me, there is a tangible risk inflation proves more difficult to tame, requiring monetary policymakers to act more assertively than is currently priced into financial markets ... [F]or me, the greater risk at present is of central bank complacency allowing the inflationary (big) cat out of the bag.

In retrospect, this sounds prescient and smart, but it is important to realise that Haldane was not persuaded – in public at least – that excessive money growth was the cause of the UK's coming setback on inflation. Like Tenreyro, he saw households' accumulated liquid savings as likely to lead to too much spending. His speeches were silent on the rapid growth of broad money, although the accumulation of liquid assets by households was merely an aspect of that. Anyhow he resigned from the Bank of England on 30 June 2021.

Too much money chasing too few assets

The eventual return of double-digit inflation to the UK surprised and bewildered almost everyone, except for the handful of economists who followed money trends. As in other nations, leaders of economic thought and numerous pundits were caught unawares. The main macroeconomic numbers turned out sharply at variance with expectations, including the expectations implicit in the market pricing of various assets.

A theme of this study is that changes in the quantity of money need to be related to national wealth as well as national income and expenditure. In particular, changes in the quantity of money affect the stock market and residential housing, and sometimes do so in ways that have profound wider consequences. By late 2020 money was growing rapidly in the UK. Was the weight of money already having noticeable positive effects on asset prices?

The stock market can be taken first, with the FTSE 100 index (30 December 1983 = 1,000) serving as a representative measure of UK share prices. On 15 February 2020 the FTSE 100 index was just under 7,400 and was close to the average value in the last two years. In the following month, to 14 March, it plunged by nearly a third to almost 5,200, as investors abandoned investments in oil companies, airlines, restaurant businesses and so on. But in the balance of 2020 share prices moved ahead and by the start of January 2021 they were less than 10% off the February 2020 peaks. The recovery may have been partly due to some switching away from US equities, which were soaring on the back of the US money supply explosion.

But an important polemical point needs to be made. By mid 2020 most people realised that the spread of Covid-19 could be checked by vaccines and that life would be back to semi-normality within a few quarters. All the same, Covid-19 was an undoubted negative for some industries and might reduce aggregate profits. The stock market should therefore have been pessimistic through late 2020 and 2021. In fact, it traded near to all-time peaks. As noted in chapters 6 and 8, the argument applied with even more force in the US. How did the resilience – even the buoyancy – of major asset classes make any sense, in view of the damage inflicted on so much of the economy by Covid? Of course, it did not make sense, unless observers noticed that the quantity of money had ballooned. If investors kept their money balances stable as a proportion of their investment portfolios, and if their money balances jumped by 50%, the value of those portfolios had also to go up by 50%.[5]

---

[5] The author has argued these points in many places, including chapter 6 in the current work (see also, for example, Congdon 2005).

House prices come next, and here also the data upset conventional thinking. The Nationwide Building Society has prepared indices of house prices, both nationally and for UK regions, since 1952. It has a quarterly series, for all houses, old and new. For present purposes the focus is on how Covid and the Covid-related money growth acceleration affected UK house prices. The natural assumption has to be that Covid was bad for the UK economy and so ought to have been bad for house prices. But that is not the apparent message of the Nationwide's data. In the two years to the first quarter of 2020 the Nationwide all-houses index increased by 2.5%. By contrast, in the two years to the first quarter of 2022 – effectively the period of the Covid pandemic – it advanced over five times more, by 12.6%. A feature of the data is that – even in late 2020, when Covid was still a source of public anxiety and the Bank of England remained nervous that monetary policy might fail to boost the economy – house prices were climbing.

Enough has been said to support the argument that UK asset price inflation was higher in the Covid period than before it. The strength of asset prices in the otherwise unhappy Covid period seems odd, but it is consistent with a condition of 'too much money chasing too few assets'. Chapter 6 emphasised that, when asset prices rise sharply, the economy is stimulated in several ways. Obviously, households feel better off and consumption benefits from a positive 'wealth effect'. A more subtle point is that companies are able to issue securities on more favourable terms, reflecting the higher prices and lower yields in the corporate financial world. The increased value of corporate fund-raising has further ramifications. It boosts the incomes of the corporate finance teams and traders involved in the fund-raising, and transfers money balances from the financial system to industrial and commercial companies. By spring 2021 official data reported an impressive increase in the amount of money held mainstream UK corporates, with the annual rate of growth matching that seen in the Lawson boom.

Too much money chasing too few goods

The year 2021 was a strange one for the British economy. Like other economies, the impact of the Covid pandemic on business activity was a diminishing influence as the months went by and vaccines became more widely available, but separating the pandemic's effects from those due to underlying economic behaviour was difficult. In the second quarter of 2020 – when the restrictions on interpersonal contact were strongest – national output, in real terms, was 21.5% down on its level in the second half of 2019. It recovered strongly in the third quarter of 2020, when it jumped by 17.5%, but then struggled to regain the previous peak levels. A May 2022 press release on monthly GDP from the Office for National Statistics reported real output in early 2022 as being little more than 0.5% up on late 2019.[6]

---

6 The sources here are press releases from the ONS. The data are revised frequently and there is surely little need for a more detailed reference.

A standard assumption in much macroeconomic forecasting is that economies have a positive and quite stable underlying trend rate of output growth. An apparently plausible interpretation of output's refusal to return to normal in 2021 and early 2022 might then be that demand was inadequate. By extension, the key policy authorities – the Treasury and the Bank of England – had failed to give enough stimulus to production. However, business surveys contradicted this interpretation. The Confederation of British Industry has conducted surveys of companies' intentions towards output and prices, and of constraints on output, as far back as 1958. It has, from the early 1960s, prepared a three-times-a-year and then quarterly survey reporting on labour shortages – both unskilled and other – as a factor limiting output. Figure 4 shows, for the last 60 years, the % balance of companies saying that difficulty recruiting the two kinds of labour was holding back production.[7] In late 2021, shortages of skilled labour were almost as severe as in the Heath–Barber boom, which had been responsible for a dreadful peak 26.9% increase in the retail price index in August 1975. Further, shortages of other kinds of labour, often unskilled, were the highest in the history of the CBI survey.

Survey evidence therefore implied that, by autumn 2021, the UK economy suffered from serious overheating. To obtain new employees, companies would have to bid harder

---

7 The author is grateful to the staff at the Confederation of British Industry who supplied him with historical data. Quarterly numbers have been interpolated for the early years, when the survey was carried out three times a year.

in the labour market, putting upward pressure on wage increases. Already global commodity prices had bounded back from their lows in March and April 2020, as the world's top economies had started to bring Covid under control. In particular, oil prices had not just overcome the worst of the shock from the interruption of travel and transport, but threatened to rise above pre-Covid levels.

Figure 4   Labour shortages, as seen by UK business, 1961–2022

% balance of companies in CBI survey citing lack of labour as a constraint on output.

Companies increasingly expressed concern about shortages of key components and production bottlenecks. These were often – but not always – due, at least apparently, to international forces. Just as business surveys indicated potential dangers of increased wage inflation quite early in the recovery from Covid, so they revealed the growing threat from rising raw material and input costs. The October 2021 quarterly survey from the CBI had a positive balance of 81% of companies expecting rising costs per unit of output in the next three months. This was the highest such positive balance since the mid 1970s. A condition of 'too much money chasing too few assets' had become generalised throughout the economy, which was now experiencing 'too much money chasing too few goods and services'.

The Great Destabilisation

In August 2021, the annual increase in the consumer price index was 3.2%, just above the top of the corridor (of between 1% and 3%) permitted by the official inflation target system. The blemish on the Bank of England's performance necessitated an open letter from its Governor to the Chancellor of the Exchequer. In the year to December 2021, the increases in the consumer price index and the retail price index were 5.4% and 7.5% respectively. Four months later – that is, for the year to April 2022 – the numbers had become 9.0% and 11.1%, again respectively. The 11.1% retail price index figure was above that in the summer of 1990, after the Lawson boom, and was the highest for 40 years. Some of the jump in inflation in early 2022 was widely attributed to an unforeseeable geopolitical shock, Russia's invasion of Ukraine on 24 February. The invasion had several side-effects on the prices of internationally traded products, with the most obvious being another increase in oil and gas prices.

All the same, inflation had moved well above target before late February. In the year to February 2022 – before any effect could have come from the Ukraine events – the consumer price index rose by 6.7%, already more than three times the target figure. The peak in the annual rate of consumer price inflation was in October, at 11.1%. In summer and autumn 2022 the figure was regularly above 10%, more than five times that envisaged in the August 2020 *Monetary Policy Report*.

The onset of high inflation created new uncertainties for households and businesses. Important issues were the duration of above-target inflation, the severity of the inevitable policy tightening as the Bank of England tried to bring inflation back to target, and the risk of recession in coming quarters. Economists wondered whether Bank rate – which had typically been 0.5% or less in the decade to 2021 – might have to be raised to 5%.[8] In the event Bank rate rose on no less than 14 occasions, from a little above zero in late 2021 to a 5.25% figure which took effect on 3 August 2023. Yields on British government securities rose sharply in 2022, partly in anticipation of the increases in Bank rate and partly to pre-empt further erosion of their real value by inflation. The cost of servicing the national debt climbed steeply. As was noted by Treasury documents accompanying the March 2022 *Spring Statement* on taxation and the public finances:

> Debt interest spending is forecast to reach £83.0 billion next year [that is, the 2022/23 financial year] – the highest

---

[8] David Milliken, Bank of England interest rate could hit 4% or more, ex-policymakers warn, *Reuters*, 11 May 2022.

nominal spending ever and the highest relative to GDP in over two decades. This is nearly four times the amount spent on debt interest last year (£23.6 billion in 2020–21) and exceeds the budgets for day-to-day departmental spending on schools, the Home Office and the Ministry of Justice combined (totalling £78.3 billion in 2022–23). Spending on debt interest in 2022–23 is £42.2 billion above the October forecast and the OBR say that the increase in the forecast for debt interest spending in 2022–23 'is also our largest forecast-to-forecast revision to debt interest on record'.

These sentences contained a dire warning about the potential unsustainability of public finances. But Cabinet ministers and Conservative MPs – egged on by several newspaper commentators – urged both tax cuts and expenditure increases, as if the budget deficit could expand indefinitely relative to national output. They seemed to believe that nations can make themselves richer by running large budget deficits. Hardly anyone declared support for a balanced budget, although this had been the guiding principle of budgetary decisions in the second half of the economically successful Conservative government from 1979 to 1997.

The Great Stabilisation had become the Great Destabilisation. Whereas in the late 2010s Britain had steady economic growth, on-target inflation, and satisfactory public finances, by late 2022 worries about a recession were widely held, inflation was far above target, and the interest bill on the public debt was soaring because of a severe loss of financial market confidence.

Who was to blame?

In 1997 the Bank of England had been granted operational independence to conduct monetary policy, in the clear understanding that it would be answerable if inflation were significantly above or beneath target. But – with inflation perhaps soon to reach more than five times the target figure – its Governor, Andrew Bailey, denied responsibility. On 16 May 2022 he gave evidence to the Treasury Committee of the House of Commons. Why had inflation taken off? Bailey said that neither he nor his colleagues at the Bank of England had done anything wrong.

Instead 'a sequence of shocks' to costs and prices had been 'unprecedented'. He cited the surge in energy prices and a supposedly 'apocalyptic' jump in food prices related to the Ukraine war, coming soon after supply-chain disruptions and 'the lingering effects' of Covid. Britain's excess inflation was due only a limited extent – 20%, according to Bailey – to domestic forces. In his view, 80% of the upward pressure on the consumer price index was driven by global circumstances outside the Bank's control.

Bailey's analysis was misleading and wrong, on at least two counts. First, rather obviously, the UK is only one member of the world economy. All the world's countries were – and remain – vulnerable to the supposed '80%' impact from global cost and price increases. But inflation rates differed dramatically between countries. In 2020, an acceleration of money growth had been seen in nearly all leading nations, as their economic policies responded to the Covid pandemic. The US led the pack, with the euro zone and the UK in the middle, Japan some way behind, and Switzerland as the slowcoach. In the year to April 2022, the period relevant as background to Bailey's 16 May appearance before the Treasury Committee, the consumer price indices in Japan and Switzerland went up by a mere 2.5%. Meanwhile inflation in the US over the *two* years to April 2022 was *above* that in the UK by about 2 percentage points and that in Switzerland by 10 percentage points. If every country is affected by the same cost influences from internationally traded commodities, and if these cost influences are such a fundamental determinant ('80%', allegedly) of inflation, why did consumer inflation vary so much between countries?

Bailey and his colleagues thought that a large and conspicuous change in relative prices – that arising, above all, from the invasion of Ukraine – excused them from paying attention to the absolute price level. It did not, and never does. If the quantity of money is held back appropriately, a big jump in energy and food prices is offset by reductions (or smaller increases) in the prices of other products and services, and the overall inflation rate stays down. A key variable here is the exchange rate. Nations that are truly committed to price stability are not afraid of currency appreciation, which will lower the prices of every import relative to what would otherwise have occurred.

The second fundamental error in Bailey's remarks was that they failed to integrate asset markets into the discussion. Over the long run a connection must hold between the prices of assets and the prices of goods and services. In the Covid-related boom–bust cycle, as in the UK's three others in the last 50 years (to recall, the Heath–Barber boom and bust, the Lawson boom and the subsequent bust inside the European Exchange Rate Mechanism, and the Great Recession cycle), a conspicuous feature was a bout of house price inflation before and during the period of excess demand. The reason in the Covid cycle, as in the others, was that too much money was chasing too few assets. Does it need to be said that Bailey's 'sequence of shocks' from the world economy cannot have any bearing on UK house prices? It would be preposterous to claim that apocalyptic rises in food prices due to the Ukraine hostilities, a lack of shipping capacity in Asia and the like were responsible for the 50% or more rises in the price of houses in Cornwall and Pembrokeshire recorded in the two years from spring 2020.

Some politicians laudably mentioned money trends in their contributions to the public debate. Liam Fox MP wrote for Conservative Home on 18 May 2022 that, while adverse global inflation pressures were relevant, the UK was being hit by 'the monetary inflation that afflicts those countries whose central banks have allowed persistent increases in the amount of money relative to existing output'. But – in the various statements emanating from the Bank of England – an egregious characteristic was the total silence on money.

Did the Bank have a theory of inflation?

In a lecture for the Institute of International Monetary Research in November 2021, Mervyn King, a former Governor now unconnected with policymaking, mentioned the omission. In his view, 'A satisfactory theory of inflation cannot take the form 'inflation will remain low because we say it will'; it has to explain how changes in money – whether directly via quantitative easing or indirectly via changes in interest rates – affect the economy.' On 13 June 2023 King, as a member of the House of Lords' Economic Affairs Committee, asked Andrew Bailey outright, 'What is your theory of inflation?' (see Bailey 2023). Like Jay Powell in Washington, the emphasis in Bailey's answer was on the balance between supply and demand in the economy, although he conceded the possible importance of 'the money impact'. He even noted that *in 2021* 'a number of people' had been exercised by 'rapid growth in the M4 aggregate'.[9]

Perhaps unfairly, some journalists felt that Bailey's answer was so diffuse that in fact he had no organised theory about inflation at all. But an argument could be made that the Bank's economists did have, and still do have, a theory. Huw Pill, who followed Haldane as chief economist, was forthright in one of his early speeches about his doctrinal preferences. As mentioned in the introduction, in an early speech he described the three-equation New Keynesian model as 'canonical' and said that a version of it guided monetary policymakers (Pill 2022b).[10] In truth Pill and his colleagues had listened to the New Keynesians and were in awe of their work. They really did believe that the impact of

---

9 Bailey did not seem to be aware that someone – that is, the author of this book – had rung the alarm bells in spring 2020.

10 Pill did caution, 'Although estimated, I would emphasise that this is a stylised representation of the UK economy – I am using it for illustrative purposes, rather than to foreshadow any specific policy decision.'

policy decisions on the economy could be measured wholly by the central bank rate and bond yields (as with the 'IS function' discussed in the introduction and in chapter 6), and, for example, that the effect of changes in the quantity of money on the stock market and house prices could be ignored altogether. (In early 2022 one of Pill's interlocutors at the Bank was Silvana Tenreyro, whose views were discussed above in chapters 5 and 6.)

Given their attitudes towards the quantity of money and the economy, they had no means of incorporating the behaviour of money in their forecasting. Several speeches and talks from MPC members in the Covid period have been quoted in the current chapter. A consistent pattern in these pronouncements was to combine neglect of the quantity of money with a tendency to comment on problems several months back as if they were still live issues. As we have seen, well into 2021 the MPC was worried that monetary policy might be unable to boost demand and output, and that deflation might become entrenched. Its members betrayed their textbook Keynesianism, by too often adverting to such fanciful pathologies as 'the zero bound' and 'the liquidity trap' (for an example, see Vlieghe 2021: 10). They were doing this even as commodity prices were surging, and UK house prices were increasing by over 0.5% a month. As noted above, a small group of private sector economists, the Shadow Monetary Policy Committee, was able to use money trends in a largely correct inflation forecast several months before the Bank of England and its key policymaking committee realised that they should be worrying about inflation, not deflation.

10 HOW THIS RESTATEMENT DIFFERS FROM FRIEDMAN'S

The version of the quantity theory of money developed in this book owes much to Milton Friedman, whose name has so far been mentioned 31 times.[1] However, it differs from his position in at least three material respects. First, the last chapter has considered the determination of the quantity of money in the Covid-affected period by looking at the credit counterparts to broad money growth. Thus, the increase in US broad money was explained in chapter 8 by the expansion of the banking system's assets, mostly (although not entirely) as a result of decisions taken by the US Federal government, the US Treasury and the Federal Reserve. The growth of the quantity of money was not related at all to the monetary base and the money multiplier. (The growth pattern of the monetary base in the UK in the relevant period was also ignored in chapter 9.) Our approach has therefore been a rejection of that favoured by Friedman for all of his long career.

---

1 Keynes's name has appeared 32 times. It makes sense for the author to be called a 'Keynesian monetarist'!

Unreliable base money multiplier

In fact, any supposed mechanical relationship between the monetary base and the quantity of money has vanished in the twenty-first century.[2] Friedman seemed to believe that a form of proportionality postulate held between the monetary base and the quantity of money, with an x% rise in the base necessarily associated with an x% increase in the quantity of money. He put his trust in a relationship of this sort in his 1959 Millar lectures in New York (Friedman 1960: 50–51), and over 20 years later in his 1980 evidence on monetary policy, given to the Treasury and Civil Service Committee of the House of Commons in the UK (Friedman 1991: 53–55). The essence of his position was that, if the central bank wanted to increase (or decrease) the quantity of money by y%, it should organise its purchases (or sales) of securities from (or to) the banking system by the requisite amount, and the desired increases (or decreases) of y% in both the monetary base and the quantity of money would eventuate.

But, awkwardly for Friedman, central banks do not work like this. They view commercial banks, in one respect, as their customers. In particular, they try to ensure that these customers have sufficient cash to be able always to repay deposits with cash. Friedman wrote as if the central bank controlled the *quantity* of the monetary base and

---

2 Much of the explanation was that central banks started in the early twenty-first century to pay interest on banks' cash reserves, which altered their attractiveness relative to other assets and their role in commercial bank balance sheets. For further details, see Selgin (2016). See also Selgin (2018).

should be indifferent to short-term interest rates, which could be left to 'market forces'. In practice, central banks control the *price* of the loans they make, with the quantity of base being allowed to vary to meet the banks' requirements. (For the author's views on the matter, see Congdon (2018).) Much more could be said about this subject, but a fair generalisation is that Friedman failed to persuade central bankers, central bank economists and most other economists of the real-world validity of his views on monetary control. The base multiplier approach to the determination of the quantity of money is rejected by most economists and not part of the current restatement of the quantity theory of money.

Blatant assault on market economy

Secondly, a leading strand in inter-war Chicago University monetary economics was the proposal that bank deposits – or at any rate bank deposits which could be used without notice – should be backed 100% by cash reserves.[3] Friedman sympathised with this suggestion, particularly in papers written early in his career.[4] But it forms no part of the restatement of monetarism now being advanced.

Friedman once co-authored a book with the title *Free to Choose* (Friedman and Friedman 1980). Its message

---

3   The proposal for 100% cash reserves against deposits was basic to the Chicago approach to monetary policy in the 1930s (see Tavlas 2023: 74–81).

4   The 100% cash reserves idea was one component of Friedman's 1948 proposed 'monetary and fiscal framework for monetary stability' (see Friedman 1953: 135–36).

was the superiority of capitalism over socialism; it argued that free choice by property-owning individuals would give better economic results than the direction of resource allocation and production by a government bureaucracy. But, in a competitive capitalist economy, banks require a loan book to earn profits from their balance sheets. Plainly, if banks' assets are to be 100% cash, they cannot have loan books and they cannot make profits from extending credit.

As far as banks are concerned, the state's imposition of the 100% cash reserve requirement would be a blatant assault on management autonomy and an existential threat to profitability. Few more radical and oppressive government interventions in a free enterprise economy could be imagined. Apparently, Friedman – like several other Chicago economists – believed that agents in a market economy should be free to choose, unless they were bankers who wanted to set their cash ratios to maximise profits subject to the well-known constraints. It must be asked, 'On what basis are banks so different from non-banks in a capitalist economy that their operations are to be subjected to intrusive regulation which would crush their profits and destroy their very reason for being?' Further, 'do Chicago School economists accept that people will invest in banking only if it receives a return on capital at least equal to that elsewhere in the economy?'[5]

---

5 Criticisms of the Chicago plan from a free-market perspective are rare, but – in the author's view – they are necessary, compelling and long overdue. Thomas Sargent (2013), the 2011 Nobel laureate in economics, also noticed the damage to banking as an industry from the Chicago plan.

Friedman's vacillations on money aggregate

Thirdly, as has been emphasised more than once, the favoured money aggregate throughout this chapter and this book is broadly defined to include nearly all of banks' deposit liabilities and, in fact, to be dominated by bank deposits. In the classic 1963 work on *The Monetary History of the United States, 1867–1960*, which Friedman co-authored with Anna Schwartz, the two authors said that 'our' concept of money was a broadly defined one including time deposits (Friedman and Schwartz 1963a: 630). This sounds consistent with the advocacy of broad money as the correct aggregate in macroeconomic analysis. However, Friedman's views in this area of the subject fluctuated during his career. During the 1970s and 1980s he often referred to the M1 narrow aggregate, perhaps because this aggregate was easier to fit into the base multiplier approach to money stock determination.[6] At one point Friedman said that the debate about the relative merits of different money concepts was unproductive, because ultimately all the aggregates moved together.[7] However, in both the Great Recession and the Covid-related business cycle the aggregates moved at wildly different rates, contradicting Friedman's observation (Congdon 2011: 252–53).

---

[6] For most of the twentieth century, under Federal Reserve rules, banks had to maintain cash reserves against sight deposits (the main constituent of M1), but not against time deposits (which became the dominant element in M2 and M3).

[7] 'The Fed has specified targets for several [money] aggregates primarily … to obfuscate the issue and reduce accountability. In general, the different aggregates move together' (Friedman 1985: 5).

The present commitment to broad money as the correct one has a vital advantage over the woolliness and imprecision on this topic which unfortunately blighted Friedman's career when he was most in the public eye. Clearly, the monetary transmission mechanism cannot be the same for narrow money and broad money. They differ in size and hence in their relationship with other macroeconomic variables, and they are held by different agents. By sticking to *one* aggregate, it has been possible to put forward *one* account of the monetary transmission mechanism. Given the widely – although falsely – rumoured opacity of the monetarist transmission mechanism, this is an important merit.

If self-described 'monetarists' refer to 'the aggregates' in the plural, the implication is that an assortment of transmission mechanisms is relevant, with distinctive nuances and angles. Questions are raised about their relative power and different ways of working. This generates confusion and uncertainty, and gives comfort to those critics – Woodford, Tenreyro and so on – when they deny the existence of a money channel altogether. Moreover, the essence of the transmission mechanism in chapters 5 and 6 was that – if a monetary disequilibrium had emerged, and if the quantity of money were a given amount for the next few periods – national income and wealth had to adjust to restore monetary equilibrium in those next few periods. Excess or deficient money was therefore *causing* changes in expenditure decisions and asset portfolios. Because of the scope for money transfers to change narrow money (as noted in chapter 2), narrow money does not have this causative property.

Friedman's most serious forecasting error, his 'blooper', came in the early and mid 1980s, as was noticed in the introduction. He predicted in his *Newsweek* column a big rise in American inflation which did not happen. The argument of the last paragraph is fundamental to understanding what went wrong. In the early 1980s, dollar interest rates fell sharply, with Fed funds rate tumbling from a peak of 19.1% in June 1981 to under 9% for much of 1983. The rise in M1 in this period was largely attributable to transfers from very high interest-earning time and wholesale deposits (which had not been in M1) to lower-return deposits inside M1. (The *relative* advantage of the very high return deposits fell sharply because of the drop in the general level of interest rates.) Also important was a side-effect of the 1980 Depository Institutions Deregulation and Monetary Control Act, which allowed the chequing accounts inside M1 to pay interest. Essentially, the high growth of M1 was due to money transfers within the broad-money total, which were prompted by changes in relative returns on different types of deposit. Such money transfers have no effect on broad money, and no necessary significance for *either* money-holders' expenditure decisions *or* their portfolio allocations between money and non-money assets. The money transfers in and out of M1 in the early 1980s did not justify an alarmist view on inflation – or indeed any view on inflation at all.

Narrow money may occasionally be a good indicator of economic conditions, but this gives it only a bit part in the transmission mechanism. Another weakness of narrow money is that it hardly fits meaningfully into discussions of portfolio selection, since the nearest alternative to a narrow money is another kind of money balance. Our account of monetary transmission has highlighted the quantitative importance of variable-income assets in household wealth and the applicability of the proportionality postulate to these assets.

11 CONCLUSION: THE QUANTITY THEORY'S CONTINUING RELEVANCE AND ANALYTICAL POWER

It is time to conclude. This restatement of the quantity theory of money has argued that its key propositions remain valid when an all-inclusive (or broadly defined) measure of money is used; it has concentrated on the monetary transmission mechanism, while also giving evidence to support the major claims. In modern circumstances the proportionality postulate is concerned with the relationship between changes in the quantity of money and changes in nominal GDP, not only changes in the price level. It has to be qualified during cycles because of the possibility of monetary disequilibrium. Further, even over the medium and long runs, strict equi-proportionality may not hold because of 'financialisation' and other factors.

A necessary and sufficient condition?

All the same, substantial bodies of evidence from numerous economies are clear that, over the medium and long run, changes in velocity are small relative to changes in both the quantity of money and nominal national income.

CONCLUSION

The statement 'large changes in the quantity of money are a necessary and sufficient condition for large changes in the nominal national income' may be an exaggeration, but it points macroeconomic discussion in the right direction. Policymakers – particularly those at the top of today's central banks – would be ill-advised to ignore it. Central banks may nowadays have a substantial degree of operational autonomy from governments and politicians, but they cannot conjure resources from thin air, and they are certainly not omnipotent.[1]

We have seen that in the final weeks of March 2020, the Federal Reserve engineered rates of increase in broad money which were much higher than the underlying trend rate of growth of US output. In the month of April 2020, M3 broad money increased by 7.4%. If that had continued for a year, the quantity of money would have climbed by 135%. The quantity theory claims that a marked acceleration in money growth will cause a marked acceleration in inflation. Does it need to be said that the laws of monetary economics are the same in North and South America?

Chapter 1 had a reference to Keynes, in which he was said to have ended by hating the quantity theory of money. Without doubt, his thought processes when writing the 1936 *General Theory* were different from those when writing the 1923 *Tract on Monetary Reform* and the 1930 *Treatise on Money*. Indeed, in the *Treatise*, Keynes explicitly said that 'formerly' he had been 'attracted' to quantity-theory

---

1 A case can be made that in the twenty-first century central banks were being asked to do too much, so that they lost sight of their priority to maintain low inflation (see Issing 2021).

reasoning, but he wanted to move on. In his view, to obtain 'real insight', we need to bring in 'the rate of interest' and 'the distinction between ... savings and investments' (Keynes 1971: 229).

Did Keynes end up 'hating' the quantity theory?

These remarks seem to foreshadow the liquidity preference theory of the rate of interest and the multiplier theory of national income determination in the *General Theory*. The two ideas – signature themes of the Keynesian revolution – were incorporated in the 1948 Samuelson textbook on *Economics* and its subsequent 19 editions. But the data on asset value changes highlighted in our chapter 6 argue that the liquidity preference theory of the rate of interest does not deserve its place in the sun. Arguably, it should be replaced by the proposition that – in equilibrium – changes in the value of variable-income assets are equi-proportional with changes in the quantity of money. After all, in late 2020, changes in the value of the variable-income assets held by American households were more than 1,000 times larger than those in the value of their bonds.

And does it need also to be recalled that the multiplier theory in the *General Theory* is about output *in real terms* and hence in employment? The *General Theory* is not about the determination of the price level and inflation, except in its rather miscellaneous penultimate book V. Moreover, the final paragraph of book V includes the remark, 'the long-run relationship between national income and the quantity of money will depend on liquidity-preferences'

(Keynes 1973: 309). If the phrase 'liquidity preferences' were replaced – very reasonably – by 'the properties of the money demand function', the proposition is the same as that developed in chapter 4 above. In other words, Keynes's preferred long-run theory of the determination of national income and output *in nominal terms* remained – even as he was finishing the *General Theory* – the inter-war Cambridge version of the quantity theory. Does this amount to hatred of the quantity theory?

In any discussion of the behaviour of the price level and nominal GDP, and of inflation in both commodities and assets, the quantity theory of money remains not just relevant, but crucial. The quantity theory of money was originally the quantity theory *of the value of money*, since its central message accords with the laws of supply and demand. If too much money is created, its value will fall, whereas – if an economy becomes short of money – its value will rise. The main propositions of the quantity theory are fundamental to any analysis of the relationship between money and inflation in the 2020s. Not only did supporters of the quantity theory score a major forecasting success in this period by their early and correct anticipation of the inflation surge. They also were able – as shown by the current work – to provide a robust theoretical underpinning for their prognoses.

APPENDIX TO CHAPTER 8

The contents of a special e-mail sent out on 30 March 2020 on 'Money trends in the US in 2020'

Sceptics and critics might say that chapter 8 is all very well, and interesting and valuable perhaps. They might also object that it has been written after the event and to that extent it lacks credibility. The author has therefore decided to add an appendix to the chapter, which reproduces much of a piece he wrote and distributed on 30 March 2020. This was a special e-mail to subscribers to the Institute of International Monetary Research, a UK-based research charity which he founded in 2014.

> Of course no one knows the exact effect of recent official decisions on US money growth in the next few weeks and months, but it is already evident that a major lurch towards monetary expansionism is under way. As just noted, my very recent suggestion [in a special e-mail about a fortnight earlier] – that broad money growth might be in the 10 per cent – 12½ per cent band by year-end – is now out-of-date. So much happened in the fortnight to Friday, 27th March, that by themselves these two weeks may have seen a 4 per cent jump in

the quantity of money, broadly defined. Moreover, this jump has occurred *before*

i. the implementation of the massive hand-outs in the CARES legislation and
ii. the Fed's indication that it will finance the budget deficit on its own balance sheet, if markets are not prepared to do so at a low enough level of bond yields.

I am reluctant to give too many hostages to fortune, and the Fed and other policymakers may have a rethink. Nevertheless, it seems entirely possible that by year-end US broad money will be 15 per cent – 20 per cent up on a year earlier. [The increase in M3 in the year to December 2020 was in fact 21.7%.] Are there any precedents? In the First World War some quarters had similar annual money growth rates, while in the Second World War the annual rate of M2 growth exceeded 25 per cent in 1943 and was also briefly above 20 per cent in late 1944/early 1945. But it is otherwise a struggle to find comparable figures in the historical record. (In the early 1970s – ahead of the notorious Great Inflation – the highest annual growth rates of M2 were just above 15 per cent.)

In other words, 2020 may well see the highest growth rates of the quantity of money in [modern] American history, apart from some exceptional quarters in the world wars of the last century. Quite probably, money growth in 2020 will be the highest ever in peacetime.

	% annual growth rate:	
	M3	Nominal GDP
1960–2018	7.4	6.5
1960–1970	7.7	6.8
1971–1980	11.4	10.3
1981–1990	7.7	7.7
1991–2000	5.6	5.6
2001–2010	7.1	3.9
Eight years to 2018	4.0	4.0

Central to the Institute's work is the relationship between the growth rates of money and nominal gross domestic product. For the US the key data are reproduced above. [The idea is the same as that behind Table 7 in chapter 7.] Notice that since 2006 the Federal Reserve has stopped preparing data on M3 and we have had to rely on numbers prepared by the economic consultancy, Shadow Government Statistics, which draws on banking data in the public domain. At any rate, the relationship between the two series is clear.

What then will be the consequences of the sharp money growth acceleration? When the coronavirus outbreak comes under control (as it surely will), the money created by the fiscal and monetary largesse of the last few weeks will still be in the economy. We are only a few months ahead of the next Presidential election, and neither senior figures in the administration nor the Fed top brass will be in any mood to withdraw the vast money stimulus. Inflation is being held down at present by the collapse in energy prices, while the annual inflation rates on which the media focus take some time to pick up any change in trend. (The increase in prices in the year to April 2021 includes the months of April, May and June 2020, when inflation pressures may have been very different in strength from those in February and March 2021.)

The money stimulus will cause asset prices to recover, and demand and output to grow rapidly, at least for a few quarters until bottlenecks are reached. The initial public response to the better news will of course be excitement and applause, not least because the recovery will be such good news after the misery of March 2020. Killjoys and skinflints, and defenders of sound money, will be ignored in the public debate.

My conclusion is that the US's economic policy response to the coronavirus outbreak will be very inflationary, even if the political situation and lags in the inflationary process will make this a concern more in 2021 (and perhaps 2022) than in 2020. Assuming that money growth does reach the 15 per cent – 20 per cent band for a few months, the message from history is that the annual increase in consumer prices will climb towards the 5 per cent – 10 per cent area and could go higher.

In short, the author

- forecast *in late March 2020* a rise in inflation to the 5 – 10 per cent area, to occur in 2021 and 2022, and
- said that this rise in inflation was the direct and predictable result of actions taken by the Federal Reserve.

Readers can decide for themselves whether these words constituted a satisfactory prognosis of the inflationary ailment that was about to hit the American economy. The words were certainly not written with the benefit of hindsight, but ahead of the developments they so accurately foretold.

REFERENCES

Bacon, R. and Eltis, W. (1976) *Britain's Economic Problem: Too Few Producers*. London: Macmillan.

Bailey, A. (2023) 13 June 2023 – Bank of England: how is independence working? Oral evidence given to the House of Lords' Economic Affairs Committee (https://committees.parliament.uk/event/18565/formal-meeting-oral-evidence-session).

Barber, W. (1997 [1935]) *The Works of Irving Fisher*, vol. 11: *100% Money*. London: Pickering & Chatto.

Barnett, W. (2012) *Getting It Wrong*. Cambridge, MA: MIT Press.

Barro, R. (1974) Are government bonds net wealth? *Journal of Political Economy* 82(6): 1095–17.

Bernanke, B. (2022) *21st-Century Monetary Policy*. New York: W. W. Norton & Co.

Bernanke, B. and Blinder, A. (1988) Credit, money, and aggregate demand. *American Economic Review* 78(2): 435–39. (Papers and Proceedings of the One-Hundredth Annual Meeting of the American Economic Association.)

Bernanke, B. and Gertler, M. (1995) Inside the black box: the credit channel of monetary policy transmission. *Journal of Economic Perspectives* 9(4): 27–48.

Blaug, M. (1985) *Economic Theory in Retrospect*, 4th edn. Cambridge University Press.

Blaug, M., Eltis, W., O'Brien, D., Patinkin, D., Skidelsky, R. and Wood, G. (1995) *The Quantity Theory of Money: From Locke to Keynes and Friedman*. Aldershot: Edward Elgar.

Bodin, J. (1997 [1568]) *Reply to the Paradoxes of Malestroit*. London: Thoemmes Continuum. (Translated by Denis O'Brien from the original *La réponse aux paradoxes de Malestroit* (1568).)

Broadbent, B. (2023) Monetary policy: prices vs. quantities. Speech given at the National Institute on 25 April 2023 (https://www.bankofengland.co.uk/speech/2023/april/ben-broadbent-speech-hosted-by-national-institute-of-economic-and-social-research). (The quotation is from the section on 'Macro models and the determination of demand'.)

Burns, J. (2023) *Milton Friedman: The Last Conservative*. New York: Farrar, Straus and Giroux.

Castañeda, J. and Congdon, T. (2020) *Inflation: The Next Threat?* London: Institute of Economic Affairs.

Clarida, R., Galí, J. and Gertler, M. (1999) The science of monetary policy: A New Keynesian perspective. *Journal of Economic Literature* 37(4): 1661–707.

Congdon, T. (1978) *Monetarism: An Essay in Definition*. London: Centre for Policy Studies.

Congdon, T. (1992) *Reflections on Monetarism*. Aldershot, UK, and Brookfield, US: Edward Elgar.

Congdon, T. (2005) *Money and Asset Prices in Boom and Bust*. London: Institute of Economic Affairs.

Congdon, T. (2007) *Keynes, the Keynesians and Monetarism*. Cheltenham, UK, and Northampton, US: Edward Elgar.

Congdon, T. (2009) *How to Stop the Recession*. London: Centre for the Study of Financial Innovation.

Congdon, T. (2011) *Money in a Free Society*. New York: Encounter Books.

Congdon, T. (2018) On some principles to fix the quantity of bank money. In *The General Theory and Keynes for the 21st Century* (ed. S. Dow, J. Jesperson and G. Tily), ch. 8. Cheltenham, UK, and Northampton, US: Edward Elgar.

Congdon, T. (2020) Will the current money growth acceleration increase inflation? An analysis of the US situation. *World Economics* 21(2): 1–24.

Congdon, T. (2021a) Interest rates or quantity of money? Edward Nelson on Milton Friedman. *Economic Affairs* 41(3): 320–35.

Congdon, T. (2021b) Can central banks run out of ammunition? The role of the money-into-equities interaction channel in monetary policy. *Economic Affairs* 41(1): 21–37.

Congdon (2021c) Does the upturn in Eurozone money growth imply 5% inflation? *SUERF Policy Note* 242. SUERF: The European Money and Finance Forum, Vienna.

Congdon, T. (2022) The modern money machine: review of Nicholas Wapshott *Samuelson Friedman*. *The New Criterion* 41(2).

Congdon, T. (2023a) *Inflation: Why Has It Come Back? And What Can Be Done?* London: Politeia.

Congdon, T. (2023b) If 'money matters', what about the monetary base? *Journal of Economic Affairs* 43(2): 185–200.

Congdon, T. (forthcoming) *Money and Inflation at the Time of Covid*. Edward Elgar.

Dow, C. (1998) *Major Recessions: Britain and the World, 1920–95*. Oxford University Press.

Emmett, R. (2010) *The Elgar Companion to the Chicago School of Economics*. Cheltenham, UK, and Northampton, US: Edward Elgar.

Fama, E. (1980) Banking in a theory of finance. *Journal of Monetary Economics* 6: 39–57.

Federal Reserve (2023) *Financial Accounts of the United States*. 2nd quarter 2023 issue, Table B103. Washington, DC: Federal Reserve.

Fisher, I. (1911) *The Purchasing Power of Money. Its Determination and Relation to Credit, Interest and Crises*. New York: Macmillan.

Friedman, M. (1953) *Essays in Positive Economics*. University of Chicago Press.

Friedman, M. (ed.) (1956) *Studies in the Quantity Theory of Money*. University of Chicago Press.

Friedman (1959) Statement on monetary theory and policy, given in Congressional briefings in 1959, reprinted in (1969) *Inflation* (ed. R. J. Ball and P. Boyle), pp. 136–45. Harmondsworth: Penguin.

Friedman, M. (1960) *A Program for Monetary Stability*. New York: Fordham University Press.

Friedman, M. (1969) *The Optimum Quantity of Money*. London and Basingstoke: Macmillan.

Friedman, M. (1985) The case for overhauling the Federal Reserve. *Challenge* (July–August): 4–12.

Friedman, M. (1991) *Monetarist Economics*. Oxford: Basil Blackwell, for the Institute of Economic Affairs.

Friedman, M. (1992) *Money Mischief*. New York: Harcourt Brace Jovanovich.

Friedman, M. and Friedman, R. (1980) *Free to Choose*. New York: Harcourt, Brace & Co.

Friedman, M. and Schwartz, A. (1963a) *A Monetary History of the United States, 1867–1960*. Princeton University Press.

Friedman, M. and Schwartz, A. (1963b) Money and business cycles. *Review of Economics and Statistics* 45(supplement): 32–64.

Galbraith, J. K. (1975) *Money: Whence It Came, Where It Went*. Boston, MA: Houghton Mifflin.

Galí, J. (2008) *Monetary Policy, Inflation and the Business Cycle*. Princeton University Press.

Goodhart, C. (2008) The boundary problem in financial regulation. *National Institute Economic Review* 206: 48–55.

Gurley, J. and Shaw, E. (1960) *Money in a Theory of Finance*. Washington, DC: Brookings Institution.

Hahn, F. (1984) *Equilibrium and Macroeconomics*. Oxford: Basil Blackwell.

Haldane, A. (2021) Inflation: a tiger by the tail? Prerecorded speech given online, 26 February 2021. Issued by the Bank of England.

Hanke, S. (2023) Monetary facts and inflation. *World Economics* 24(3): 19–26.

Hicks, J. (1982) Money, interest and prices. In *Collected Essays on Economic Theory* (J. Hicks), vol. II, ch. 23. Oxford: Basil Blackwell.

Hicks, J. (1989) *A Market Theory of Money*. Oxford University Press.

Hoover, K. (1988) *The New Classical Macroeconomics: A Sceptical Enquiry*. Oxford, UK and Cambridge, MA: Basil Blackwell.

IMF (2023) *World Economic Outlook*, April 2023 database, accessed in September 2023. Washington, DC: International Monetary Fund.

Issing, O. (2021) Central banks – independent or almighty? SAFE (Safe Architecture for Finance in Europe), policy letter 92. Frankfurt: Leibniz Institute for Financial Research.

REFERENCES

Kaldor, N. (1982) *The Scourge of Monetarism*. Oxford University Press.

Keynes, J. M. (1971 [1930]) *The Treatise on Money*, vol. 1: *The Pure Theory of Money*. In *The Collected Writings of John Maynard Keynes* (ed. E. Johnson and D. Moggridge), vol. V. London and Basingstoke: Macmillan for the Royal Economics Society.

Keynes, J.M. (1972 [1933]) *Essays in Biography*. In *The Collected Writings of John Maynard Keynes* (ed. E. Johnson and D. Moggridge), vol. X. London and Basingstoke: Macmillan for the Royal Economics Society.

Keynes (1973 [1936]) *The General Theory of Employment, Interest and Money*. In *The Collected Writings of John Maynard Keynes* (ed. E. Johnson and D. Moggridge), vol. VII. London and Basingstoke: Macmillan for the Royal Economics Society.

Laidler, D. (1991) *The Golden Age of the Quantity Theory*. New York and London: Philip Allan.

Laidler, D. (2002) The quantity theory of money. In *An Encyclopaedia of Macroeconomics* (ed. B. Snowdon and H. Vane), pp. 603–7. Cheltenham, UK, and Northampton, US: Edward Elgar.

Mankiw, G. (2019) *Macroeconomics*, 10th edn. New York: Macmillan International.

Marshall, A. (1922) *Money, Credit and Commerce*. London: Macmillan.

Mayer, T. (1980) David Hume and monetarism. *Quarterly Journal of Economics* 95(1): 89–101.

Mill, J.S. (1900) *Principles of Political Economy*, 6th edn (new impression). London: Longman, Green and Co.

Mirowski, P. (2013) *Never Let a Serious Crisis Go to Waste*. London, UK and New York, US: Verso.

Nelson, E. (2020) *Milton Friedman and Economic Debate in the United States, 1932–72*. University of Chicago Press.

Patinkin, D. (1965) *Money, Interest and Prices*, 2nd edn. New York: Harper & Row.

Pepper, G. and Oliver, M. (2006) *The Liquidity Theory of Asset Prices*. Chichester: John Wiley & Sons.

Penn Wharton Budget Model (2020) The long-run fiscal and economic effects of the CARES Act. Blog post, 5 May 2020 (https://budgetmodel.wharton.upenn.edu/issues/2020/5/5/long-run-economic-effects-of-cares-act).

Pill, H. (2022a) What did the monetarists ever do for us? Speech given at Inflation and Debt: Challenges for Monetary Policy after Covid-19, Walter Eucken Institut / Stiftung Geld und Währung Conference (https://www.bankofengland.co.uk/speech/2022/june/huw-pill-speech-at-the-walter-eucken-institute).

Pill, H. (2022b) Monetary policy with a steady hand. Speech given at the Society of Professional Economists online conference, 9 February 2022. Issued by the Bank of England.

Polak, J. (1957) Monetary analysis of income formation and payments problems. *IMF Staff Papers* 6(1): 1–50.

Romer, D. (2000) Keynesian macroeconomics without the LM curve. *Journal of Economic Perspectives* 14(2): 149–69.

Samuelson, P. (1972) *The Collected Scientific Papers of Paul Samuelson*, vol. 3. Cambridge, MA: MIT Press.

Samuelson, P. (1948) *Economics*, 1st edn. New York: McGraw-Hill.

Sargent, T. (2013) Drawing lines in US monetary and fiscal history. In *The Economic Crisis in Retrospect* (ed. G. P. West III and R. Whaples). Cheltenham, UK, and Northampton, US: Edward Elgar.

Schumpeter, J. (1981 [1954]) *History of Economic Analysis* (12th impression). London: George Allen & Unwin.

Schwartz, A. (1987) *Money in Historical Perspective*. University of Chicago Press.

Selgin, G. (2016) Interest on reserves and the Fed's balance sheet. Testimony to Congressional Sub-Committee on Financial Services, Monetary Policy and Trade, 17 May 2016 (https://www.cato.org/publications/testimony/interest-reserves-feds-balance-sheet#).

Selgin, G. (2018) *Floored!: How a Misguided Fed Experiment Deepened and Prolonged the Great Recession*. Washington, DC: Cato Institute.

Senate Committee on Banking, Housing and Urban Affairs (2021) *Semi-Annual Policy Report to the Congress*, 21 February 2021. Washington, DC: Government Printing Office.

Skidelsky, R. (2018) *Money and Government*. Penguin Random House.

Skousen, M. (1992) The trumpet gives an uncertain sound. In *Dissent on Keynes* (ed. M. Skousen), ch. 1, pp. 9–34. New York and Westport: Praeger.

Smialek, J. (2023) *Limitless*. New York: Alfred Knopf.

Steel, G. (2014) The credit counterparts of broad money: a structural base for macroeconomic policy. Lancaster University Management School Economic Working Paper Series 4.

Stracca, L. (2007) Should we take inside money seriously? ECB Working Paper Series 841. Frankfurt: European Central Bank.

Stracca, L. (2010) Is the New Keynesian IS curve structural? ECB Working Paper Series 1236. Frankfurt: European Central Bank.

Sumner, S. (2021) *The Money Illusion: Market Monetarism, the Great Recession, and the Future of Monetary Policy*. University of Chicago Press.

Tavlas, G. (2023) *The Monetarists*. University of Chicago Press.

Tenreyro, S. (2021) Responses to the Covid-19 pandemic: UK and US experiences. Lecture to the Federal Reserve Bank of San Francisco spring conference, 26 March 2021, issued by the Bank of England.

Tenreyro, S. (2023) Quantitative easing and quantitative tightening. Speech given at the Scottish Economic Society annual conference, 4 April 2023 (https://www.bankofengland.co.uk/speech/2023/april/quantitative-easing-quantitative-tightening-speech-silvana-tenreyro). (The quotation comes from the section 'QE is an asset swap'.)

Tobin, J. (1971) *Essays in Economics*, vol. 1: *Macroeconomics*. Amsterdam: North Holland.

US Department of the Treasury (2022) *The Future of Money and Payments* (https://home.treasury.gov/system/files/136/Future-of-Money-and-Payments.pdf). Washington, DC: US Treasury.

Vlieghe, G. (2021) An update on the economic outlook. Speech at Durham University, 22 February 2021, issued by the Bank of England.

Walters, A. (1971) *Money in Boom and Slump*, 3rd edn. London: Institute of Economic Affairs.

Weber, M. (2013 [1921]) *Economy and Society* (ed. G. Roth and C. Wittich). Berkeley, CA: University of California Press. (Originally published 1921 as Wirtschaft und Gesellschaft.)

Wicksell, K. (1935) *Lectures on Political Economy* (translated from Swedish by E. Classen), vol. II: *Money*. London: George Routledge and Sons.

REFERENCES

Wicksell, K (1936) *Interest and Prices: A Study of the Causes Regulating the Value of Money* (translated from German by Richard Kahn). London: Macmillan for the Royal Economic Society.

Woodford, M. (2003) *Interest and Prices: Foundations of a Theory of Monetary Policy.* Princeton University Press.

Woodford, M. (2010) Financial intermediation and macroeconomic analysis. *Journal of Economic Perspectives* 24(4): 21–44.

ABOUT THE IEA

The Institute of Economic Affairs is a research and educational charity (No. CC 235 351). Its mission is to improve understanding of the fundamental institutions of a free society by analysing and expounding the role of markets in solving economic and social problems.

The IEA achieves its mission through:

- a high-quality publishing programme
- conferences, seminars, lectures and other events
- outreach to school and university students
- appearances across print, broadcast and digital media

The IEA, established in 1955 by the late Sir Antony Fisher, is an educational charity, not a political organisation. It is independent of any political party or group and does not carry on activities intended to affect support for any political party or candidate in any election or referendum, or at any other time. It is financed by sales of publications, conference fees and voluntary donations.

In addition to its main series of publications, the IEA publishes the academic journal *Economic Affairs* in partnership with the University of Buckingham.

The IEA is aided in its work by an Academic Advisory Council and a panel of Honorary Fellows. Together with other academics, they review prospective IEA publications, their comments being passed on anonymously to authors. All IEA papers are therefore subject to the same rigorous, independent refereeing process as used by leading academic journals.

IEA publications are often used in classrooms and incorporated into school and university courses. They are also sold throughout the world and often translated and reprinted. The IEA supports and works with a global network of like-minded organisations, through its Initiative for African Trade and Prosperity, EPICENTER and other international programmes.

Views expressed in the IEA's publications are those of the authors, not those of the Institute (which has no corporate view), its Managing Trustees, Academic Advisory Council members or senior staff. Members of the Institute's Academic Advisory Council, Honorary Fellows, Trustees and Staff are listed on the following page.

The Institute gratefully acknowledges financial support for its publications programme and other work from a generous benefaction by the late Professor Ronald Coase.

The Institute of Economic Affairs
2 Lord North Street, Westminster, London SW1P 3LB
Tel: 020 7799 8900
Email: iea@iea.org.uk
Web: iea.org.uk

Executive Director and Ralph Harris Fellow	Tom Clougherty
Editorial Director	Dr Kristian Niemietz

Managing Trustees
Chair: Linda Edwards
Kevin Bell
Professor Christian Bjørnskov
Robert Boyd
Robin Edwards
Tom Harris
Professor Patrick Minford
Bruno Prior
Professor Martin Ricketts

Lord Vinson – Life Vice President and former Chair of the IEA Board of Trustees
Professor D R Myddelton – Life Vice President and Former Chair of the IEA Board of Trustees

Academic Advisory Council
Chair: Professor Martin Ricketts
Dr Mikko Arevuo
Graham Bannock
Dr Roger Bate
Professor Alberto Benegas-Lynch, Jr
Professor Christian Bjørnskov
Professor Donald J Boudreaux
Professor John Burton
Professor Forrest Capie
Dr Juan Castaneda
Professor Steven N S Cheung
Dr Billy Christmas
Professor David Collins
Professor Tim Congdon
Professor Christopher Coyne
Professor David de Meza
Professor Kevin Dowd
Professor David Greenaway
Dr Ingrid A Gregg
Dr Samuel Gregg
Professor Steve H Hanke
Professor Keith Hartley
Professor Peter M Jackson
Dr Jerry Jordan
Professor Syed Kamall
Professor Terence Kealey
Dr Lynne Kiesling
Professor Daniel B Klein
Dr Benedikt Koehler
Dr Mark Koyama
Professor Chandran Kukathas
Dr Tim Leunig
Dr Andrew Lilico
Professor Stephen C Littlechild

Dr Matthew McCaffrey
Professor Ted Malloch
Dr Eileen Marshall
Dr John Meadowcroft
Dr Anja Merz
Dr Lucy Minford
Professor Patrick Minford
Professor Julian Morris
Professor Alan Morrison
Professor D R Myddelton
Dr Marie Newhouse
Dr Chris O'Leary
Paul Ormerod
Dr Neema Parvini
Professor Mark Pennington
Professor Srinivasa Rangan
Dr Alex Robson
Professor Pascal Salin
Dr Razeen Sally
Professor Pedro Schwartz Giron
Professor J R Shackleton
Professor Jane S Shaw Stroup
Professor W Stanley Siebert
Shanker Singham
Professor Andrew Smith
Dr Carlo Stagnaro
Professor Elaine Sternberg
Professor James Tooley
Professor Nicola Tynan
Professor Roland Vaubel
Dr Cento Veljanovski
Professor Lawrence H White
Professor Geoffrey E Wood

Honorary Fellows
Professor Michael Beenstock
Professor Richard A Epstein
Professor David Laidler

Professor Deirdre McCloskey
Professor Vernon L Smith

Other books recently published by the IEA include:

Top Dogs and Fat Cats: The Debate on High Pay
Edited by J. R. Shackleton
ISBN 978-0-255-36773-8; £15.00

School Choice around the World ... And the Lessons We Can Learn
Edited by Pauline Dixon and Steve Humble
ISBN 978-0-255-36779-0; £15.00

School of Thought: 101 Great Liberal Thinkers
Eamonn Butler
ISBN 978-0-255-36776-9; £12.50

Raising the Roof: How to Solve the United Kingdom's Housing Crisis
Edited by Jacob Rees-Mogg and Radomir Tylecote
ISBN 978-0-255-36782-0; £12.50

How Many Light Bulbs Does It Take to Change the World?
Matt Ridley and Stephen Davies
ISBN 978-0-255-36785-1; £10.00

The Henry Fords of Healthcare ... Lessons the West Can Learn from the East
Nima Sanandaji
ISBN 978-0-255-36788-2; £10.00

An Introduction to Entrepreneurship
Eamonn Butler
ISBN 978-0-255-36794-3; £12.50

An Introduction to Democracy
Eamonn Butler
ISBN 978-0-255-36797-4; £12.50

Having Your Say: Threats to Free Speech in the 21st Century
Edited by J. R. Shackleton
ISBN 978-0-255-36800-1; £17.50

The Sharing Economy: Its Pitfalls and Promises
Michael C. Munger
ISBN 978-0-255-36791-2; £12.50

An Introduction to Trade and Globalisation
Eamonn Butler
ISBN 978-0-255-36803-2; £12.50

Why Free Speech Matters
Jamie Whyte
ISBN 978-0-255-36806-3; £10.00

The People Paradox: Does the World Have Too Many or Too Few People?
Steven E. Landsburg and Stephen Davies
ISBN 978-0-255-36809-4; £10.00

An Introduction to Economic Inequality
Eamonn Butler
ISBN 978-0-255-36815-5; £10.00

Carbon Conundrum: How to Save Climate Change Policy from Government Failure
Philip Booth and Carlo Stagnaro
ISBN 978-0-255-36812-4; £12.50

Scaling the Heights: Thought Leadership, Liberal Values and the History of The Mont Pelerin Society
Eamonn Butler
ISBN 978-0-255-36818-6; £10.00

Faith in Markets? Abrahamic Religions and Economics
Edited by Benedikt Koehler
ISBN 978-0-255-36824-7; £17.50

Human Nature and World Affairs: An Introduction to Classical Liberalism and International Relations Theory
Edwin van de Haar
ISBN 978-0-255-36827-8; £15.00

The Experience of Free Banking
Edited by Kevin Dowd
ISBN 978-0-255-36830-8; £25.00

Apocalypse Next: The Economics of Global Catastrophic Risks
Stephen Davies
ISBN 978-0-255-36821-6; £17.50

New Paternalism Meets Older Wisdom: Looking to Smith and Hume on Rationality, Welfare and Behavioural Economics
Erik W. Matson
ISBN 978-0-255-36833-9; £12.50

An Introduction to Taxation
Eamonn Butler
ISBN 978-0-255-36836-0; £12.50

Imperial Measurement: A Cost–Benefit Analysis of Western Colonialism
Kristian Niemietz
ISBN 978-0-255-36839-1; £10.00

Other IEA publications

Comprehensive information on other publications and the wider work of the IEA can be found at www.iea.org.uk. To order any publication please see below.

Personal customers

Orders from personal customers should be directed to the IEA:

IEA
2 Lord North Street
Westminster
London SW1P 3LB
Tel: 020 7799 8911
Email: accounts@iea.org.uk

Trade customers

All orders from the book trade should be directed to the IEA's distributor:

Ingram Publisher Services UK
1 Deltic Avenue
Rooksley
Milton Keynes MK13 8LD
Tel: 01752 202301
Email: ipsuk.orders@ingramcontent.com

IEA subscriptions

The IEA also offers a subscription service to its publications. For a single annual payment (currently £42.00 in the UK), subscribers receive every monograph the IEA publishes. For more information please contact:

Subscriptions
IEA
2 Lord North Street
Westminster
London SW1P 3LB
Tel: 020 7799 8911
Email: accounts@iea.org.uk